Presented to

_____

From

_____

Date

_____

HEIRLOOM

Living and Leaving a Legacy of Faith

KATHY HOWARD

Tyndale House Publishers
Carol Stream, Illinois

LIVING EXPRESSIONS
COLLECTION

Living Expressions invites you to explore God's Word in a way that is refreshing to the spirit and restorative to the soul.

Visit Tyndale online at tyndale.com.

TYNDALE, Tyndale's quill logo, *Living Expressions*, and the Living Expressions logo are registered trademarks of Tyndale House Ministries.

Heirloom: Living and Leaving a Legacy of Faith

Designed by Jacqueline L. Nuñez

27   26   25   24   23   22   21
7   6   5   4   3   2   1

Contents ✦

*I could have no greater joy than to hear that
my children are following the truth.*

3 JOHN 1:4, NLT

Introduction ✍

I'm fascinated by the stories of my ancestors. I want to know where they came from, how they lived, and what they were like. Their stories help me understand how I got to be "me." Maybe you feel the same way.

The Bible places great value on knowing our family history, specifically our spiritual roots. The stories of those who have come before us can strengthen and encourage our faith today. As we live intentionally for God, we lay a spiritual foundation for those who come after us.

When our three children were growing up, my husband and I worked to encourage their faith. In hindsight, I see some gaps in our discipling. We could have been more purposeful in some areas. Looking toward the future, I want to take advantage of every opportunity God gives us with our grandchildren.

What legacy do you want to leave for your children, grandchildren, and great-grandchildren? For other members of your extended family? The most valuable heirloom we can pass down is a legacy of faith. While we can't believe *for* any of our loved ones, we can teach them about our great God and create an atmosphere in our homes where trust in him can flourish. We can tell our own stories, share God's Word, and point them to Jesus.

This devotional book is designed to help you purposefully live today in ways that will leave a legacy of faith for your descendants. *Heirloom* ties the past to the future. Within these pages are fifty-two stories about people who have gone before us and how they lived and whom they worshiped. These stories, which come from personal anecdotes, historical records, and the Bible, reveal the seeds of our faith—seeds that sprouted and took root, growing through the centuries to touch our lives today.

These accounts exemplify biblical principles of spiritual legacy. Each devotion includes Scripture, questions for personal reflection, a prayer, and a practical tip to help you create a spiritual heirloom your family will treasure. And if you love digging into the stories of your own family's past, each devotion includes a bonus genealogy research tip.

Today we're reading our ancestors' stories. Tomorrow our descendants will be reading our stories. What kind of legacy will we leave?

Kathy Howard

1 A Prayer from My Great-Great-Grandmother

This is my prayer: that your love may abound more and more in knowledge and depth of insight, so that you may be able to discern what is best and may be pure and blameless for the day of Christ.

PHILIPPIANS 1:9-10

I found a treasure while cleaning out a desk at my parents' home. Stuffed in an old metal box, it shared the space with a pair of delicate, wire-rimmed spectacles and a small ledger with regular entries of twenty-five cents a week in savings. The letter, yellowed and fragile with age, was dated March 26, 1914. I struggled to read the faded ink. Addressed to Howell Adam Shouse, my great-grandfather on my mother's side, it was written by his mother, Mary Dozier Shouse.

Much of the news was what you'd expect—who had been sick, who had gotten married, who had visited, and how she longed to see her "dear son." But one paragraph brought me to tears:

Oh, how much I do pray for you every single morning and night. I pray mightily to the Lord that you, Howell, and your children may be convicted and converted and sanctified. Never a day do I miss. May God hear and answer my prayers.

In chapter 1 of the apostle Paul's letter to the Christians in Philippi, he recorded a similar prayer for their spiritual well-being. Paul loved these "spiritual children" and prayed for them constantly.

Like Paul, Mary Dozier Shouse faithfully interceded on behalf of her descendants. This discovery thrilled me, because I knew her prayers covered me too. Long before I was born, my great-great-grandmother prayed for me to have a saving, growing relationship with Jesus. The letter challenged me not just to pray for the physical welfare of my loved ones, but also to faithfully lift prayers that matter for eternity.

Yes, I pray for my family's physical circumstances. But I pray for their spiritual needs and struggles as well. Maybe one day my great-great-granddaughter will find my prayer journal and be blessed when she discovers that I prayed for her.

READ PHILIPPIANS 1:3-11 AND REFLECT: What kinds of things did Paul prayerfully request for the Philippian Christians? How can you use this prayer and others in Scripture as models for praying for the spiritual well-being of your family and friends?

Father, thank you for the incredible privilege of connecting with you through prayer. May I faithfully bring my family by name before you. Teach me how to specifically pray for them in ways that matter for eternity. In Jesus' name, amen.

Legacy Tip

Make a list of Scriptures you can pray for your loved ones. Regularly let your family know the things you are praying for them. Send texts and emails often, but also drop them a handwritten note when possible. In addition, consider keeping prayer journals that will encourage your family long after you have gone to be with Jesus.

Genealogy Tip

OLD LETTERS, POSTCARDS, AND OTHER CORRESPONDENCE

Living before the digital age, your ancestors used pencils or pens and paper to communicate. Letters, cards, journals, and other materials, written by and between your ancestors, are valuable sources for genealogical research. They can provide a treasure trove of clues about family members. If you have old correspondence, it is a good idea to digitize each item to preserve them for future generations. You might also choose to share them online so other researchers can benefit from your findings. Archivists recommend removing old letters from envelopes and leaving them unfolded, as continuous unfolding and refolding causes wear to the creases and could eventually tear the paper. Store the original letters and postcards in archival-quality sleeves for safekeeping. Pay particular attention to postmarks and stamps since they provide clues about the time periods and locations of your ancestors.

2 | Lingering Melody

Give praise to the Lord, proclaim his name;
make known among the nations what he
has done. Sing to him, sing praise to him;
tell of all his wonderful acts.

PSALM 105:1-2

When Becky was a child, she took piano lessons. As she got older, her life filled with other commitments and she found less time for the creative outlet. Now, after a forty-year hiatus, her love for the instrument has reawakened. She loves to worship God through music, continuing a family legacy that spans four generations.

It began in a small country church in North Florida, where Becky's great-grandmother Lizzie McIntosh was the church pianist. Lizzie found assurance of heaven and God's care for her through the words in the old hymns. "Blessed assurance, Jesus is mine! O what a foretaste of glory divine," Lizzie played and sang, offering God a sacrifice of praise. "Praise him! Praise him! Jesus, our blessed Redeemer! Sing, O earth, his wonderful love proclaim!"

Sadly, in 1914, at the age of twenty-eight, Lizzie died during childbirth. She left behind a husband, three small children, and an invalid father-in-law. She also left a lingering melody of praise. Her graceful accompaniment and sweet singing had planted seeds in the heart of her nine-year-old daughter, Rubye. Those seeds sprouted and grew into an avid love for the piano.

Like her mother, Rubye faithfully served in the church and led many friends and family members to Christ. And also like her mother, she passed on a passion for music to her daughter, Elizabeth—Becky's mother. Now an octogenarian, Elizabeth still enjoys playing songs from her church's hymnal. The music Elizabeth plays is a call to worship in the style of Psalm 105, urging God's people from all generations to praise him for who he is and what he has done.

Today Becky is a dedicated piano student, always challenging herself to learn something new. When she sits at the keyboard, she experiences overwhelming joy and deep satisfaction. Part of that comes from remembering who helped mold her into the person she is today: Pianist. Daughter of the Most High. A woman who leans on the promises of eternal life with Christ.

READ PSALM 105:1-6 AND REFLECT: What guidance does this passage give for how to praise God? What attributes of God can you praise him for today? What "wonderful acts" have you experienced that you are grateful for? God deserves your worship every day, not just on Sundays. How can you foster a lifestyle of worship?

> *Father, help me explore creative ways to worship you. Fill my heart with gratitude and my mouth with praise. Inspire my family to be grateful people who are always ready to praise you. We want others to know how much we love you. In Jesus' name, amen.*

Legacy Tip

Introduce praise and worship into your family's lifestyle. Help them recognize attributes of God for which you can praise him. Incorporate music, either with a family musician or by playing praise music tracks.

Genealogy Tip

LOCATING VITAL RECORDS

Pivotal occasions mark every individual's life—key events like birth, marriage, and death. "Vital records" are the government documents that report these critical events. Some common types include birth certificates, death certificates, marriage licenses, divorce decrees, and wills. You can search for vital records at the local, county, and state levels. Hospitals and funeral homes may also hold death records. Churches or the minister who performed a marriage ceremony may have copies of marriage records. The time period and location will impact the exact formats of these records.

God's greatness   PSALMS 96-99.

shew forth his salvation from day to day.
3 Declare his glory among the heathen, his wonders among all people.
4 For the LORD *is* great, and greatly to be praised: he *is* to be feared above all gods.
5 For all the gods of the nations *are* idols: but the LORD made the heavens.
6 Honour and majesty

11 Light is sown for the rig gladness for the upright in h
12 Rejoice in the LORD, ye and give thanks at the rem his holiness.

PSALM 9
A Psalm,
O SING unto the

Exhortation to   PSALM

PSALM 100.
A Psalm of praise.
MAKE a joyful noise unto the LORD all ye lands.
2 Serve the LORD with gladness: com before his presence with

3 A Mother's Immeasurable Influence

These commandments that I give you today are to be on your hearts. Impress them on your children. Talk about them when you sit at home and when you walk along the road, when you lie down and when you get up.

DEUTERONOMY 6:6-7

O ver his lifetime, he prayed with thirteen sitting US presidents. He shared the gospel with more than 200 million people in hundreds of live crusades around the world. Hundreds of millions more heard him through the airwaves.[1] And it's estimated that more than two million people gave their lives to Christ through his preaching.[2] Although the ministry of Reverend Billy Graham cannot be encapsulated with mere numbers, these statistics emphasize the incredible impact he made during his lifetime for the Kingdom of God.

But long before Billy Graham preached the Good News to the world, his mother wove its truth into the daily fabric of his life. In his autobiography, *Just As I Am*, Billy described how his mother, Morrow Coffey Graham, gathered her family together daily to pray, read the Bible, and experience the presence of God. Her commitment to establish a family altar began the day she married William Franklin Graham Sr., and it never wavered. Morrow believed her family's eternal life and earthly unity depended on the Word of God, so she faithfully taught her children to revere Scripture.

Although Billy Graham's ministry reached well beyond his North Carolina roots, he readily acknowledged the crucial part his mother played in his life. Billy recognized the great potential every mother has to point their children to Christ, saying, "The influence of a mother upon the lives of her children cannot be measured."[3]

God designed the family to be our first and greatest school of spiritual formation. Mothers and fathers are the teachers, and the Bible is their textbook. In Deuteronomy 6, God instructs parents to weave the commandments he has given them into the patterns of family life. He commands them to teach his Word, talk about his Word, and apply his Word throughout the day—from the first awareness of morning until sleep closes in at night—and all the countless moments in between. The eternal value of this lifestyle is immeasurable.

READ DEUTERONOMY 6:4-9 AND REFLECT: What responsibility has God given us for our families regarding his Word? What command does God give in verse 5? How could obedience to that command naturally lead into your responsibility to share God's Word with your children? What are some ways you can purposefully weave God's truth into the fabric of family life?

Lord, show me how to diligently teach your Word to my family. Help me to prioritize their spiritual well-being over the demands of daily life. In Jesus' name, amen.

Legacy Tip

Establish and commit to a regular family devotion time. Shape it according to the ages and attention spans of your children. Make it fun and inter-active, and give everyone an opportunity to contribute.

Genealogy Tip

START WITH A BIRTH CERTIFICATE

Birth certificates contain significant information about ancestors. These documents include the date of birth and, usually, the child's name. Some specific situations could have prevented recording the name. For instance, the parents may not have chosen the name before the certificate was recorded, or sadly, they may have decided not to name the child if the infant lived only a few days. Birth certificates often include other information, such as the place of birth, number of siblings, and name of the "informant," the person who informed, or provided, the information. The certificates may also include more details, such as the mother's maiden name and the parents' names, their ages at the time of the child's birth, and their dates and places of birth.

4 A Stranger's Gift

I am not ashamed of the gospel, because it is the power of God that brings salvation to everyone who believes.

ROMANS 1:16

In mid-nineteenth-century England, an illiterate orphan named John Monkhouse didn't have much hope for a promising future. But no one thought to mention that to John.

Born in 1841 in London, his parents died when he was still a small boy. Although he was legally in the care of his older married sister, John spent more time roaming the city than he spent at home, playing on the streets and hanging around in the alleys where men gathered to gamble. He scrutinized the gamblers, fascinated by their games of chance. Was this what the future held for young John?

One day, a stranger changed the trajectory of John's life when he handed him a heavy black Bible. John used that Bible to teach himself how to read, and God used that Bible to bring John into a saving relationship with Jesus. From that time on, John centered his life on God and his purposes.

At sixteen, John married his fifteen-year-old sweetheart, Elizabeth. In 1871, the family immigrated to the United States, and John settled his family in Shreveport, Louisiana. John was smart and industrious. He started businesses and bought land. But John also longed to serve God. He joyfully studied the Bible to learn how to build his life and his family on God's principles. He opened his home to strangers, donated land for a new church, and faithfully told others about God and his great blessings.

God used one simple act—a gift from a stranger—to establish the foundation for a family's legacy of faith. Generations of believers, humble church leaders, and even a local church grew on that foundation.

John's great-granddaughter Jamie looks forward to a heavenly meeting with the unknown stranger whose gift on the streets of London led to an orphan's ultimate salvation. Perhaps Jamie will get to share with him how God used that one small act to impact generations.

READ ROMANS 1:11-17 AND REFLECT: Search this passage for all the ways the gospel of Christ can impact your life today and into eternity. Do you use scriptural principles to guide every life decision you make as well as your interactions with your family? If not, why not? Will you make that commitment today?

Father, I confess that too often I've used my own "wisdom" to make pivotal decisions in my life. Forgive me for not seeking your counsel. Help me to set an example for my family in my words and my deeds, an example that is based on your Word. In Jesus' name, amen.

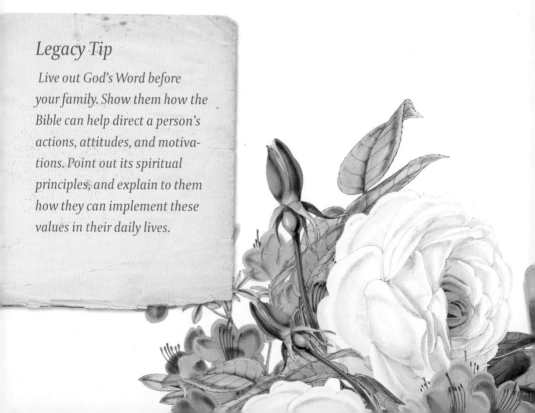

Legacy Tip

Live out God's Word before your family. Show them how the Bible can help direct a person's actions, attitudes, and motivations. Point out its spiritual principles, and explain to them how they can implement these values in their daily lives.

Genealogy Tip

NORTHERN- AND WESTERN-EUROPEAN IMMIGRANTS

Did any of your ancestors immigrate to America from Europe? One of the largest early non-English speaking groups to arrive were Germans, with their numbers peaking at the end of the nineteenth century.[4] Between 1870 and 1900, almost 12 million people emigrated from Northern and Western Europe. Many left to escape famines, land and job shortages, and heavy taxation.[5] The majority came from Great Britain, Ireland, and Scandinavian countries.[6] About 70 percent of these new arrivals entered the country either through the Castle Garden train depot in Manhattan or through the Ellis Island processing center located in New York Harbor, which opened in 1892. Check passenger lists (both immigration and emigration) through the National Archives at New York City, https://www.archives.gov/nyc/finding-aids/passenger-lists.html.

5 | Chickens, Eggs, and a Cheerful Giver

Remember this: Whoever sows sparingly will also reap sparingly, and whoever sows generously will also reap generously. Each of you should give what you have decided in your heart to give, not reluctantly or under compulsion, for God loves a cheerful giver.

2 CORINTHIANS 9:6-7

Kelley, mother of eight-year-old Micah, is using the egg business to teach her son about responsibility, money management, and tithing. The Irwins have two roosters and almost thirty laying hens that produce dozens of eggs every week—much more than their family can eat. Micah gathers and sells the extra eggs.

Micah's tasks include cleaning the coop, replenishing the poultry's food and water, and purchasing some of the less-expensive supplies. From his earnings, Micah tithes 10 percent and puts 20 percent into a long-term savings account. His parents match each deposit their son makes. Micah also chooses to save some money each month to use for Christmas and birthday gifts for his family.

When Micah dropped the white tithing envelope into the church offering plate for the first time, he experienced what his mother had told him about—the joy of giving back to God a portion of what God had given him. Kelley learned this biblical truth from her father.

In her early teens, when Kelley began babysitting to earn spending money, her dad taught her the spiritual principles of giving. She learned that God gives abundantly to her so she can give to others; that God is the source of everything we have, even our ability to work; that God provides for the needs of generous believers; that giving pleases and glorifies God; that giving demonstrates active trust in God; and that heartfelt generosity generates joy in the giver.

Kelley also learned to make giving a priority by setting aside her tithe before she spent any of what she earned. That's what her father always did, and that's what Kelley has taught Micah to do as well. If he has any money left over, Micah says he might buy some books for himself.

READ 2 CORINTHIANS 9:6-12 AND REFLECT: What does this passage teach about giving? How does giving build our faith and deepen our relationship with God?

Lord God, everything I have comes from you, including my ability to work, the job I have, and the money I earn. Help me to find joy in giving and to explore ways to stretch my gifts even further. I want to set a good example for my family. In Jesus' name, amen.

Legacy Tip

Through word and example, teach your children what the Bible says about giving to the church and to people in need. Begin showing them at an early age how to give small amounts from their weekly allowance or cash gifts they've received. If they are old enough to have jobs, discuss possible organiza-tions, ministries, or individuals they could support.

Genealogy Tip

US CENSUS REPORTS

Your ancestors have been counted! The Constitution of the United States mandates that every resident of the country must be counted through a nationwide census every ten years. The first US census began in 1790. Census records document the names and details of the population in each community, and genealogical researchers can access these records to prove the approximate date of birth, race, occupation, place of residence, and relationships of the individuals within a household. Prior to 1850, census reports generally only included the name of the head of household. Tick marks designated other family members. Sadly, we are missing at least one census record: On January 10, 1921, a fire at the US Commerce Department destroyed most of the 1890 census. Only a few fragments survived.

6 | Country Revivals and Answered Prayer

I am reminded of your sincere faith, which first lived in your grandmother Lois and in your mother Eunice and, I am persuaded, now lives in you also.

2 TIMOTHY 1:5

During the second week of August 1917, God finally answered the fervent prayers Flora Ray Davis had uttered over many years.

Flora had married Confederate Civil War veteran Francis Marion Davis in 1889. Together they raised cotton and nine children in the sparsely populated countryside of northern Louisiana. Francis was hard-working and industrious, and he taught these qualities to his children. In addition to farming, he owned and ran a sawmill, cotton gin, gristmill, and blacksmith shop that not only met his family's needs but also benefited his neighbors.

According to an account written by her youngest child, Lucelia, Flora was "a devout Christian who believed in the power of prayer." She tirelessly cared for the house and garden, made all the family's clothing, and "filled their home with joy." But the spiritual condition of Flora's husband and children kept her on her knees.

Lucelia reflected that before the yearly revival meeting of 1917, only two of the nine children had accepted Jesus as their Savior. And Francis, who struggled to control his temper and his tongue, had been "excluded from the church years before for cursing."

In the days leading up to the anticipated event, Flora and other church members prayed fervently for God to work. By the end of the week-long revival, fifty-five people had committed their lives to Jesus, including the rest of Flora's children. God also worked in Francis's heart, and in time, the church reinstated him as a member. Lucelia ended her written account with a prayer of her own: "I thank God for my parents and the Christian home they made for us."

After her parents died, Lucelia inherited the family home and, together with her husband, raised three daughters there. The Davis family's spiritual heritage continues to be passed down to each generation.

READ 2 TIMOTHY 1:3-7 AND REFLECT: In what ways did Timothy's mother and grandmother, as well as his spiritual father, Paul, encourage his faith? What are some specific ways you can instill a love for and knowledge of God in your family? How can you encourage each person's spiritual growth?

Father, my family knows that I believe in you. Help me to be a bold witness to them. Give me the words that will turn their hearts to you. In Jesus' name, amen.

Legacy Tip

Pray for your family members' spiritual well-being, not just their physical well-being. Consistently pray for their salvation, their desire to know God, their spiritual growth, boldness in their faith, and self-control in their daily lives. Pray also that they will find God's specific direction for their lives.

Genealogy Tip

CHURCH MEMBERSHIP RECORDS

Faith played a big role in the daily life of the American colonists. Beginning about 1700, many Christian denominations were established in the colonies. Congregations of Presbyterians, Catholics, Anabaptists, Mennonites, Quakers, Anglicans, Dutch and German Reformed, and Lutherans sprang up. Church records include helpful information like membership rolls, marriages, births, deaths, migration information, and minutes from monthly meetings. The Quaker Church, also known as The Society of Friends, have digitized their records and made them available on many genealogy websites.

7 | From Everything to One Thing

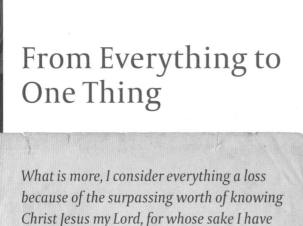

What is more, I consider everything a loss because of the surpassing worth of knowing Christ Jesus my Lord, for whose sake I have lost all things. I consider them garbage, that I may gain Christ.

PHILIPPIANS 3:8

The loss of everything can be devastating ... or it can be life changing. It all depends on a person's perspective.

Eugene and Esther Erny served God as missionaries in China for more than a decade. In 1936, something happened that forever changed their perspective on life and faith. One night, while the couple and their two young sons slept soundly in their home, a fire broke out within the missionary compound. Inside the compound's walls, a few students were huddled together, praying through the night. When they spotted the danger, they awakened everyone with urgent cries of "Fire, fire!" Eugene ensured that all the missionaries, students, and Chinese workers escaped safely. Then Esther and Eugene joined them, holding little Bobby's hand and carrying three-month-old Edward in his wicker basket.

The fire swept quickly through the compound, destroying everything. All the family's cherished possessions, household goods, and important papers were gone. Only one thing survived the fire—a handful of diapers Esther had grabbed on her way out. But no one lost their life. Every person was safe. That joy far outweighed the loss of material things.

And yet God used the fire to carry out his purposes. First, the shared loss caused the Ernys and the Chinese workers to develop a deeper bond. Second and more importantly, God used the experience to do some heart work in Eugene and Esther. They realized they had placed too much value in their possessions. Now those things were nothing but rubble and ashes. Through the flames, God taught them what was truly important.

The Ernys never forgot this lesson. Their grip on possessions was broken. Vangie, the daughter born to them after the fire, was raised in a home where she was taught to hold things loosely and to hold Jesus tightly.

READ PHILIPPIANS 3:7-11 AND REFLECT: Compared to the value of knowing Jesus, how did the apostle Paul feel about material things and accomplishments? Do an honest self-evaluation. What do you value most? Is there anything that hinders your desire for Jesus? Is there a possession or activity you need to let go of in order to know Jesus more fully?

Lord, root out all the greed, envy, and materialism from my heart and mind. Help me to desire Jesus more than anything else. I want my family to see him reflected in me. In his name, amen.

Legacy Tip

Encourage your family members to hold their possessions loosely. Live simply instead of accumulating things. Help your children protect themselves against greed, envy, and materialism.

Genealogy Tip

NATURALIZATION RECORDS

Did your immigrant ancestor become a US citizen? "Naturalization" is the process by which a foreign-born person becomes a citizen of the United States. Though not every immigrant became a citizen of his or her new country, many immigrants to America desired to become citizens. In the 1800s and early 1900s, many laws governed the naturalization process for immigrants to America. A certificate of naturalization, which is different from an immigration record, documents the end result of this process. You can look for these records on the National Archives website. There you will see a sample of the process using documentation for Maria von Trapp, made famous by her family's story in the 1965 movie *The Sound of Music*.

8 Soldier, Servant, Man of Faith

Join with me in suffering, like a good soldier of Christ Jesus. No one serving as a soldier gets entangled in civilian affairs, but rather tries to please his commanding officer.

2 TIMOTHY 2:3-4

Rebecca Price Janney is an author and historian whose Easton Series is set during the American Revolution and the twenty-first century. The novels feature two main characters—Colonel Peter Kichline and his fictional descendant. The Colonel happens to be a real-life Revolutionary War hero and even more intriguing, Janney's sixth great-grandfather.

Born in Germany in 1722, Peter Kichline immigrated to Pennsylvania in 1742, eventually settling in the newly created village of Easton in Northampton County. Fully committed to his community, Peter was actively involved in education and politics and served two terms as the county's sheriff.[7] His faith in God undergirded all he did and stood for.

He was instrumental in ensuring Easton had its first dedicated church building, helping with the cost of constructing the German Reformed Church where he served as a ruling elder.

Historically, Peter Kichline is best known for his role in the American Revolution, namely when he commanded the Northampton County Flying Camp. This was a military formation of rapid responders, which George Washington utilized during the second half of 1776. In August of that year during the Battle of Brooklyn, Peter was wounded and taken prisoner by the British. They held him for six months until he was paroled to Easton pending a prisoner exchange.[8]

After completing a term as county commissioner in 1780, Peter remained committed to his community and his country. He served as a county judge and Easton's first chief burgess, as well as a member of Pennsylvania's first constitutional convention.[9]

Rebecca Price Janney uses her extensive knowledge of this period and her genealogical research about Peter Kichline to bring her stories to life, inspired by her ancestor's deep faith and commitment to service. Peter's

example encourages Rebecca to serve others even when it makes her life more difficult.

READ 2 TIMOTHY 2:1-7 AND REFLECT: How do Paul's metaphors of a soldier, athlete, and farmer help you understand the nature of true discipleship? What did Paul say should be the aim of a soldier of Christ? Does your life reflect these characteristics to your family?

Father, show me where my discipleship is the weakest and fortify me with your strength. I want to be a true soldier of Christ who holds the banner of the gospel high. In Jesus' name, amen.

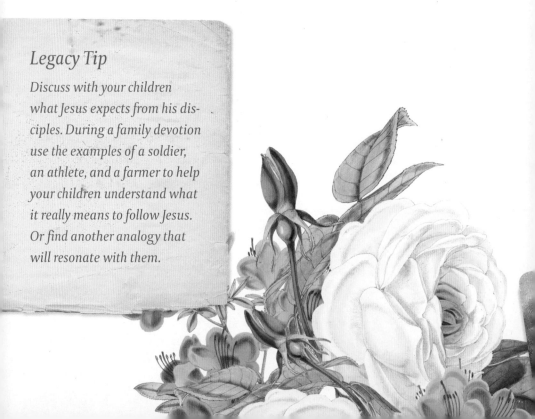

Legacy Tip

Discuss with your children what Jesus expects from his disciples. During a family devotion use the examples of a soldier, an athlete, and a farmer to help your children understand what it really means to follow Jesus. Or find another analogy that will resonate with them.

Genealogy Tip

MILITARY SERVICE RECORDS

Did an ancestor of yours serve in the military? The National Archives in Washington, DC, houses the country's military records. The transcripts and abstracts that make up the compiled military service records include basic information, such as payrolls and muster rolls, from a soldier's military career. The records organize the soldiers' names by military unit or the state of service. Find federal military service records from the Revolutionary War to the year 1912 in the National Archives. Look for military records from WWI to the present in the National Military Personnel Records Center (NPRC) at https://www.archives.gov/personnel-records-center/military-personnel. You can also search for state militia records in the archives of the respective state the soldier was from.

9 He Was a Carpenter

*Jesus grew in wisdom and stature, and
in favor with God and man.*

LUKE 2:52

Jesus worked with his hands. He cut wood and shaped it into useful objects. While he worked, he may have cut a finger, smashed his thumb, or gotten splinters. Presumably he developed calluses and got dirt under his fingernails. And those beautiful hands, the ones that drove many nails, would also be pierced by them.

Our Savior was a tradesman. The Bible identifies Jesus as a carpenter (Mark 6:3). Joseph, his stepfather, taught Jesus the family business. Imagine the amount of time the two spent together at the workbench, sawdust clinging to their clothing, talking and laughing together over their work. Joseph was the teacher, the expert, and Jesus was his young apprentice, the pupil.

Jesus learned, grew, and developed like any other child. And like any other child, Jesus needed parents to help him. God the Father chose Joseph the carpenter to be Jesus' earthly father. It wasn't happenstance; Joseph's role in Jesus' life was just as divinely deliberate as Mary's. After all, Joseph would be our Savior's role model, counselor, and guide.

Carpentry wasn't the only thing shared between father and son. Perhaps Joseph was the one who stretched out his arms and encouraged Jesus to take his first steps. I would imagine he taught Jesus how to be a good neighbor, a kind sibling, and a thoughtful friend. Maybe Joseph taught Jesus how to fish. He showed his young son how to navigate the world. Ironically, Joseph modeled for the Son of God how to be a godly man.

Joseph may not have been Jesus' biological father, but he was a good father to his son. He carefully followed the law and kept the Jewish customs. He exhibited strong character and deep trust in God. He was sensitive to God's leading and quick to respond. And Joseph fully obeyed God, even when it was difficult and costly. Maybe that radical obedience reminds you of Someone.

READ MATTHEW 1:18-25 AND REFLECT: What does the passage teach you about Joseph's character? Why do you think God chose Joseph to be Jesus' earthly father? What character traits and qualities do you need to work on, in order to be the parent or stepparent God wants you to be?

Lord God, my children are a gift from you, and I know it's important for me to be a godly example for them. May I guide them to become more Christlike. In Jesus' name, amen.

Legacy Tip

Be intentional about molding your children's character. Begin by strengthening your own godly character—being a good role model will help them. Use real-life examples to explain what good character looks like and doesn't look like.

Genealogy Tip

ELDERLY FAMILY MEMBERS

If you wait too long, you may miss hearing part of your family's story. Conduct an informal interview with the older members of your family. Prepare a list of questions beforehand. Take old letters, photos, yearbooks, and inherited items with you to spark their memories. Use a journal to record stories and specific information about locations, names, and military service. Recording the interview is another great way to preserve the story as well as your relative's voice. If you have enough information to compose a written narrative about an ancestor, post it on online genealogy sites so that everyone can access it.

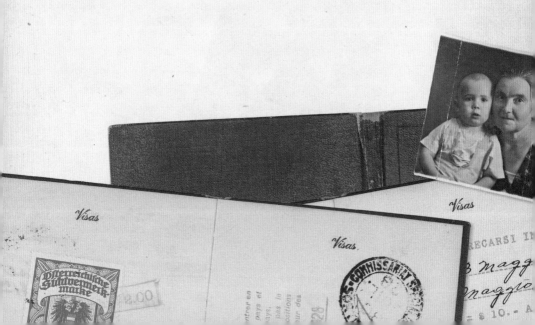

10 | Wild Hogs, Tobacco, and Skipping Church

God so loved the world that he gave his one and only Son, that whoever believes in him shall not perish but have eternal life.

JOHN 3:16

Thomas Farley was already at odds with the law and the church for drunk and disorderly conduct. But in 1626, when the colonist missed Sunday services for three months in order to hunt wild hogs, the trouble intensified. Missing church was serious business in colonial Virginia. The court found him guilty and imposed a fine of one hundred pounds of tobacco.[10] The fine padded the public treasury and restored Thomas to good spiritual status with the church.

Thomas and his wife, Jane, had sailed on the *Anne* from Worcester, England, and arrived in James City County, Virginia, in 1623. Their first child, Ann, was born either during the journey from England or shortly after landing and was named for the sailing vessel. The family settled in Archer's Hope, across the James River from Jamestown, and grew to fifteen children.

Overall, Thomas was a productive member of the community. As a landowner, he produced large quantities of tobacco for the English markets. Between 1629 and 1632, he also served two terms in the Virginia House of Burgesses.

When Julie began researching her ancestors, she hoped to find noble people—men and women of strong faith. When she first discovered Thomas Farley in her maternal family tree, she thought she'd found that honorable ancestor. Yet as she learned more about his life, she was reminded of a deep spiritual truth: Everyone falls short of God's perfection. Every person who has ever lived—every ancestor and every descendant—is a sinner (Romans 3:23) who deserves eternal separation from God (Romans 6:23).

But, praise God, there is good news. Jesus Christ willingly paid the penalty for all sins, from all time, on the cross. Eternal salvation is available to everyone as a free gift from God. Anyone who puts their faith in

Jesus and trusts in his death on the cross as the only way of salvation will spend eternity with him. Jesus is the honorable hero of every family tree, ensuring that a heritage of grace can abound for all who claim his incomparable gift.

READ JOHN 3:16-18 AND REFLECT: Have you received Jesus' gift of eternal salvation? If not, why not do so today? Admit to God that you are a sinner. Believe that Jesus is the way, the truth, and the life, the one who bore your sin on the cross. Confess him as Lord and Savior, and determine to live for him.

> *Jesus, thank you for your incredible gift of salvation, offered to everyone. Embolden me to share the gospel message every chance I get, especially to my family. I ask you to open their hearts so they will make you Lord of their lives. Amen.*

Legacy Tip

Pointing your family members to saving faith in Jesus is the most important legacy you can leave. Make the gospel of Jesus the foundation of your life and prioritize sharing the Good News with your entire family, no matter how young or old they are.

Genealogy Tip

BRITISH ROYALTY

Are you descended from kings? Some genealogical studies suggest that almost every person descended from seventeenth-century British colonists has in their ancestry one or more British monarchs. The majority of these colonial-era Brits settled in Virginia or Massachusetts. Lists of British monarchs are readily available online. As you research your family tree, look for titles of nobility such as "Sir," "Count," or "Duke." Also learn about common royal surnames and check to see if any pop up among your ancestors.

God's greatness   PSALMS 96-99.

shew forth his salvation from day to day.
3 Declare his glory among the heathen, his wonders among all people.
4 For the LORD *is* great, and greatly to be praised: he *is* to be feared above all gods.
5 For all the gods of the nations *are* idols: but the LORD made the heavens.
6 Honour and

11 Light is sown for the rig gladness for the upright in h
12 Rejoice in the LORD, ye and give thanks at the rem his holiness.

PSALM 9
A Psalm.

Exhortation to   PSALM

PSALM 100.
A Psalm of praise.

MAKE a joyful noise unto the LORD all ye lands.
2 Serve the LORD with gladness:

11 | She Chose Life

This is good, and it is pleasing in the sight of God our Savior, who desires all people to be saved and to come to the knowledge of the truth.

1 TIMOTHY 2:3-4, ESV

Elizabeth was sixteen, unmarried, and pregnant. Although this would be a difficult situation in any generation, it was especially hard in 1931. Though abortion wasn't legal at the time, Elizabeth found a physician who was willing to perform one on her. It seemed like the only solution. But when she arrived for the procedure, Elizabeth couldn't go through with it and instead chose to give her baby life.

When her son, John, was still an infant, Elizabeth's older brother, Jim, found faith in Christ during a short stint in jail. Jim then introduced Elizabeth to his Savior, and she joyfully embraced Jesus. Elizabeth's salvation changed the direction of her life and laid the foundation for John's later acceptance of Jesus.

Jesus came first in Elizabeth's life. On one occasion she had been putting aside money for a much-needed new winter coat when she became aware of a poor missionary family. Elizabeth gave them all of her savings and wore her old coat for another season. She remained faithful with her finances, and God always met their needs.

With Elizabeth's encouragement, John's faith grew vibrant and strong. Today, he longs for everyone to know his Savior. Everywhere he goes, he tells others about Jesus—in airports, at gas stations, on family vacations, and in daily interactions. He never misses an opportunity to share the Good News. John also invests time and resources in mission work, such as ongoing construction projects and Bible distribution in Mexico. And he does what he can to support single mothers.

Like his mother before him, John sets a godly example for his own family of five children, twenty-five grandchildren, and thirty-six great-grandchildren. Because Elizabeth chose the hard path more than eighty years ago, sixty-six people have physical life today. And because her son tells everyone he encounters about Jesus, countless people have spiritual life.

READ 1 TIMOTHY 2:1-7 AND REFLECT: What type of life should Christians live in their communities? What does God desire for all people? In what ways can this truth shape your interactions with people you encounter every day?

> *Lord God, you are a loving Savior who doesn't want anyone to perish for eternity. Give me a burden for the lost and a zeal to share the Good News of Jesus. In his name, amen.*

Legacy Tip

Be enthusiastic about telling others what God has done for you. The importance you put on evangelism will impact your children. Teach them about God's desire for all people to know him. Allow your children to see and hear you share the gospel with people you encounter.

Genealogy Tip

DEATH CERTIFICATES: A RICH SOURCE OF INFORMATION

In 1910, the United States government standardized death certificates. Prior to that time, death records were typically kept by churches or court-houses. In addition to the date of death, a death certificate may contain the cause and location of death, the name of the funeral home or under-taker, and the place of burial. You may also find the individual's birth date, place of birth, and marital status. Although the parents' names and birth locations may be included, this information is considered secondary evidence, since the person who provided these details may have been relying on his or her memory.

12 | Hospitality House

After Paul and Silas came out of the prison, they went to Lydia's house, where they met with the brothers and sisters and encouraged them.

ACTS 16:40

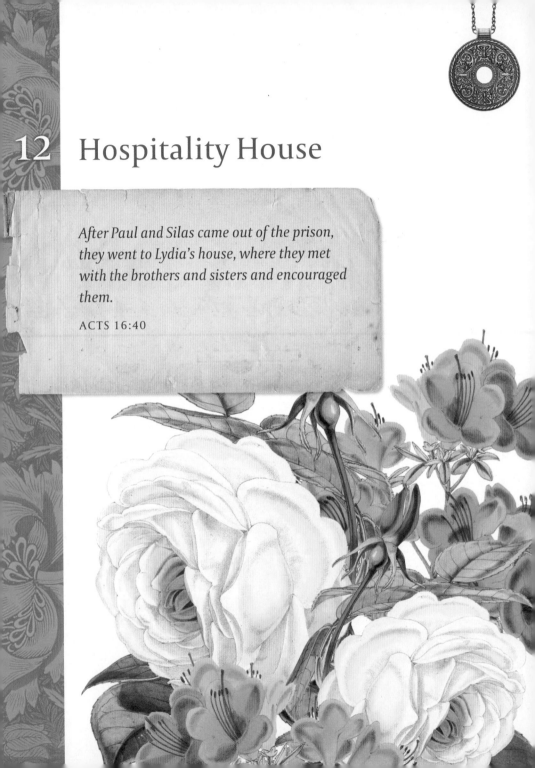

The bedroom smoke detector woke John and Sherry Gremillion at 3:30 a.m. Every alarm in the house was blaring. Smoke filled the dark room, yet a strange glow shone through the bedroom window.

"Smoke! The house is on fire! Get your parents and the dogs and call 911!" John yelled. "We've got to get out—now!"

Her parents were already halfway down the stairs as Sherry ran into the kitchen to grab her phone. As everyone—including the dogs—headed out the front door, she dialed 911.

Even though flames already filled much of the house, everyone made it safely outside. In the wee hours of the morning, they stood on the street in their pajamas and watched the red-orange blaze consume the roof of their home. The three-alarm fire was so intense, it took the firefighters more than two hours to get it under control. By the time the ordeal was over, John and Sherry's home was a blackened shell. The bulk of their possessions were gone.

Friends and neighbors quickly rallied to extend to John and Sherry the same sweet hospitality they'd received from the couple countless times through the years. The Gremillions' house was not simply their home—it was also their place of ministry. From hosting casual dinners and get-togethers to women's neighborhood Bible studies and the church small group, Sherry and John were always ready to accommodate. They welcomed and served everyone.

Now in their time of need, others served them. One neighbor took them into her home. Many others worked to provide for their basic immediate needs, such as clothes, shoes, food, and transportation.

The Gremillions' ministry echoes the pattern of hospitality modeled in Scripture. Lydia, the first-century seller of purple cloth who came to faith through Paul's message, is one example. Her first act as a newly baptized believer was to welcome Paul and his missionary companions as guests in her home. Lydia also opened her home to the new Philippian congregation.

Hospitality encourages individuals, builds up the church, and advances the gospel message. That's why the Gremillions made it a priority. After the loss of their home, many who had been blessed by John and Sherry took up the baton. And as soon as the Gremillions are settled into a new home, it will be open for ministry too.

READ ACTS 16:11-15 AND REFLECT: What was Lydia's first act of service after becoming a believer in Jesus? Do you open your home to others as quickly as Lydia did? What needs do you know of right now in your church or community that you could meet by opening your home?

Lord, I confess that I've used busyness as an excuse for not opening my home to others. Help me to obey you in this way and to get my family involved as well. In Jesus' name, amen.

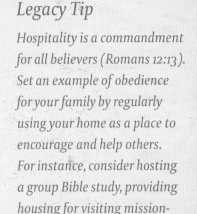

Legacy Tip

Hospitality is a commandment for all believers (Romans 12:13). Set an example of obedience for your family by regularly using your home as a place to encourage and help others. For instance, consider hosting a group Bible study, providing housing for visiting missionaries, or throwing a party for your church's youth group.

Genealogy Tip

MARRIAGE RECORDS

Do you need to prove the marriage of your ancestors? Several types of documents can help, including marriage bonds, marriage licenses, marriage applications, and marriage certificates. However, don't rely on a marriage bond alone. If that's the only record you've located, the ceremony may not have happened. Marriage bonds, often used in the 1800s and earlier, only declared the couple's *intention* to marry. The prospective groom and a bondsman posted the marriage bond, along with the bond money, as a guarantee that the marriage would be legal. The bondsman was a male relative of the groom, such as a father, brother, uncle, or cousin. These documents were more like an official engagement. They provided an opportunity for others to raise any objections against the marriage. Sometimes these intended marriage ceremonies never took place.

13 | One Voice

Perhaps the reason he was separated from you for a little while was that you might have him back forever—no longer as a slave, but better than a slave, as a dear brother.

PHILEMON 1:15-16

Harriet Beecher Stowe was born in 1811 into a godly family. Her father, Lyman Beecher, was a prominent minister who preached antislavery sermons and urged his children to give their lives to Jesus. His faith, beliefs, and convictions left their marks. All seven of his sons became ministers, and Harriet used a pen to challenge America's conscience.

Although opportunities for women were limited in the early nineteenth century, Harriet was well educated and fell in love with writing. Bolstered by her husband's encouragement, Harriet published more than thirty books and numerous articles during her lifetime. But one book she authored sent shock waves around the world.

Burdened by the injustice and immorality of slavery, Harriet used her God-given talent of writing to raise awareness of the issue. Her most famous work, *Uncle Tom's Cabin*, exposed the harsh realities and cruelty of slavery in America. Published in 1852, the book generated empathy for slaves and encouraged others to add their voices to Harriet's in the growing antislavery movement.

In a time when women could not hold office or even vote, Harriet powerfully expressed her thoughts and beliefs through her words. As an advocate for the voiceless, she was heard by her generation and beyond.

In the first century, Paul was an advocate for a man who belonged to a mistreated segment of society. Onesimus, a runaway slave, met Paul and came to faith in Christ through his testimony. Paul wrote to Philemon, Onesimus's owner, and urged him to graciously accept Onesimus not as a slave, but as a brother in Christ.

Paul not only challenged the societal norms, he also appealed to Philemon to do the same by freeing Onesimus and embracing him in mercy and grace. Paul used his voice to fight for God's justice.

READ PHILEMON 1:8-18 AND REFLECT: In what way did Paul act as an advocate for Onesimus? Is God prompting you to speak out on an issue or to use your voice to encourage other Christians? Ask God to show you how you can use your voice for his glory and others' good.

Jesus, use my voice, my time, and my resources as your tools to uplift and challenge other Christians, our society, and especially my family, to further your justice in this world. Amen.

Legacy Tip

Have a discussion with your family about injustice in today's world and the God-given inherent value of all people. Consider ways you and your family can speak out and fight for justice in a particular area. For example, you could volunteer, donate to a specific cause, and write to your representatives.

Genealogy Tip

TRACING ENSLAVED ANCESTORS

Are you looking for information about enslaved ancestors? The slave schedules published along with the 1850 and 1860 censuses are not your only source of information. Check newspapers from the pre–Civil War and Civil War eras in the American South. These papers often contained notices of slave sales and reports of runaway slaves. Since freed slaves often took on the surname of their former owners, try searching for those surnames. The Digital Library of Georgia is an excellent searchable database of old newspapers from this time period. The 1870 census was the first one to include African Americans by name, along with the rest of the population.

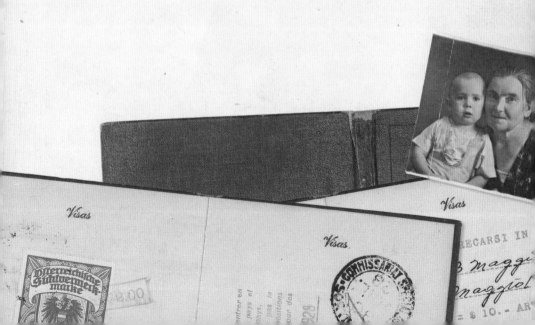

14 Passion Forged in Persecution

We have the prophetic word more fully confirmed, to which you will do well to pay attention as to a lamp shining in a dark place, until the day dawns and the morning star rises in your hearts.

2 PETER 1:19, ESV

ugo Freer's unwavering commitment to God's Word set the course of his life. Hugo was born around 1640 in Normandy, France, to a Roman Catholic family. But sometime in his teens, he became convinced of the supremacy and sufficiency of Scripture and converted to Protestantism.

It was a dangerous time to reject the authority and traditions of the Catholic Church. Throughout the seventeenth and eighteenth centuries, wave after wave of persecution threatened the French Protestants. Along with thousands of these "Huguenots," Hugo fled France to escape persecution. His deeply held convictions fueled his flight. Legend recounts that Hugo was smuggled into Germany in a barrel.[11] In his newly adopted country, he found safety—and a wife named Marie who also had fled from France.

Hugo and Marie had two daughters and a son. Tragically, around 1666 Marie and both the girls succumbed to the plague.[12] Hugo married again, and he and Jeanne Wibau had three sons together. In 1675, the family set sail on the Dutch ship *The Spotted Cow*, seeking a new life and religious freedom in the American colonies. In New York, Hugo connected with other Huguenots and helped found the New Paltz settlement near the Catskills. This small community then established a French Protestant church, where Hugo served faithfully until his death in 1698. Hugo Freer took to heart the apostle Peter's admonition to base his life on the authority and reliability of Scripture. He clung to Scripture as the source for spiritual truth and taught his children to do the same. This legacy flowed through the centuries to Jessica, Hugo's tenth great-granddaughter. She discovered his story during high school when she began researching her family history. Jessica stands on the supremacy and sufficiency of Scripture, following in the footsteps of her brave ancestor.

READ 2 PETER 1:16-21 AND REFLECT: Are you convinced of the authority of Scripture? How did Peter become convinced? What truths does this passage teach about God's Word? Based on the nature of Scripture, what place does it deserve in your life?

Father, help me adopt a personal attitude of gratitude. May I express continuous thankfulness. In Jesus' name, amen.

Legacy Tip

Demonstrate to your family your respect for and dependence on God's Word. Regularly share with them what God is teaching you through Scripture and how it guides your life. Discuss with your children what it means when you say that the Bible is "inspired by God," and emphasize Scripture's rightful place of authority in their lives.

Genealogy Tip

AGRICULTURE, INDUSTRY, AND MANUFACTURING SCHEDULES

Was one of your ancestors a farmer? Maybe another owned a factory or a mill? Research non-population census records to find more information about them and their work. These types of schedules were made to verify people involved in agriculture, industry, and manufacturing. An agriculture schedule lists the heads of households, amount of farmland owned, and the value of the land or other assets owned by the individual. Industry and manufacturing schedules may provide information about owners of factories and mills, as well as the types of goods they produced. These documents help establish that a person was in a definite location at a specific time.

15 The Whistle Stop

Oh give thanks to the LORD; call upon his name; make known his deeds among the peoples! Sing to him, sing praises to him; tell of all his wondrous works!

1 CHRONICLES 16:8-9, ESV

A train whistle always stops Lloyd in his tracks. No matter where he is or what he's doing, when he hears the whistle blow, Lloyd pauses to thank God. Sometimes his prayer is a simple "Thank you, Lord." Other times, he pauses longer to praise God and thank him for specific acts of mercy and grace in his life.

The seed for Lloyd's "gratitude prompt" was planted long ago during happy childhood days spent on his grandfather's Arkansas farm. One of Lloyd's most vivid memories of that time was the sound of the logging train that regularly chugged across the property. Thankfulness filled those days—thankfulness for his strong, gentle grandfather and his example of love and family devotion. Lloyd naturally connected those feelings of gratitude with the sound of the train.

Now, decades later, train tracks run parallel to the western border of Lloyd's Wyoming ranch in the foothills of the Bighorn Mountains. Everyone who visits the ranch hears the story of the train, its whistle, and what it reminds Lloyd to do. From family and friends to neighbors and the Wounded Warrior veterans Lloyd often hosts, everyone pauses to thank God when the whistle blows.

When King David triumphantly brought the Ark of the Covenant back to Jerusalem, he encouraged the people of God to express their gratitude. He urged Israel to remember everything God had done and to thank him for all his wondrous works. Like David, Lloyd knows that continuous gratitude fosters a deeper awareness of God and greater joy in a worshiper's heart.

Although thanking God is not hard, it is easy to forget to do. Lloyd notes, "People don't take time to stop and thank God for all he's done. We all need a little reminder."

READ 1 CHRONICLES 16:8-12 AND REFLECT: In this passage, what did David encourage God's people to do? Which phrases encourage you to tell others about God's deeds? Spend a few moments thanking God for all his "wondrous works" in your life. Make a list of at least five things God has done for you, and nudge your family to do the same.

Father, forgive me for not counting my blessings. I realize that each day— and everything in it—is a precious gift from you. May I never run out of reasons to thank you. I want my family to notice the difference in me. In Jesus' name, amen.

Legacy Tip

Develop a family "gratitude prompt" by deciding together what everyday sight or sound will remind you to thank God for his many gifts. Set a regular time for your family—perhaps around the dinner table—to recount the Lord's "wondrous works" with each other.

Genealogy Tip

THE NATURALIZATION ACT OF 1790

The Naturalization Act of 1790 was the first statute in the United States to enact a uniform rule for naturalization. This law established narrow criteria for citizenship. Only those who were white, male, and owned property could apply. The act stated the "alien" must be a "free white person" who had been in the United States for two years. Women, nonwhite persons, slaves, and indentured servants were not eligible to become citizens. Noncitizens had very limited rights. They could not own property, hold public office, or vote.

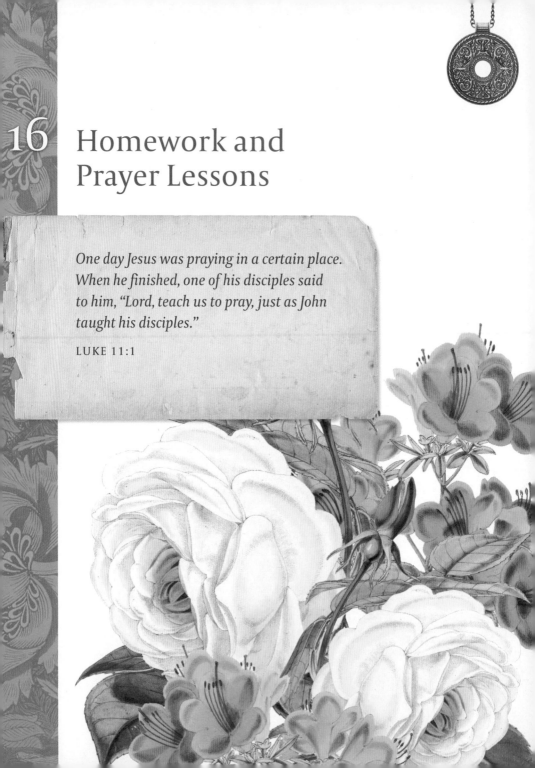

16 Homework and Prayer Lessons

One day Jesus was praying in a certain place. When he finished, one of his disciples said to him, "Lord, teach us to pray, just as John taught his disciples."

LUKE 11:1

When Sheri was just eight years old, her mother passed away. By the time she reached her teenage years, her father had remarried. Conditions in Sheri's home were difficult, and when tensions escalated, her father decided the best solution was to send the fifteen-year-old away to a school a thousand miles from home. For three years, Sheri lived with a pastor and his wife, Kay, while she attended the Christian school where Kay taught third grade.

At the end of each school day, Kay needed to grade papers and prepare the next day's lessons. So Sheri spent her afternoons at Kay's mother's house, which was right next door to the school. "Gammy" May's gentle spirit and gracious nature made Sheri feel welcomed, but it was the older Christian's passionate love for Jesus and dynamic prayer life that Sheri wanted to emulate.

When Gammy prayed, her face shone with sweet adoration for her Savior. Her prayers flowed naturally throughout the day, one moment bubbling to the surface and the next running quietly underground. Gammy prayed for family members, neighbors, and the community. She prayed for missionaries and ministers. All the while, Gammy shared her prayers and God's abundant answers with Sheri.

Looking back, Sheri realizes she learned more after school than she did during the school day. Although Gammy did not consider herself her mentor, she filled that role by teaching Sheri about the power of prayer. In her presence Sheri learned that prayer is not a passive religious ritual—it is an active spiritual weapon to help her fight on the frontlines. Gammy was a warrior, and Sheri wanted to follow her into battle.

Today, Sheri fights on her knees. God often gives her specific prayer missions, bringing names and circumstances to mind. Sometimes the compulsion to pray is so strong she is unable to do anything else until

God lifts the burden. God granted Sheri's prayer: She's a warrior, just like Gammy May.

READ MATTHEW 6:7-14 AND REFLECT: God already knows your every need before you go to him in prayer. How does this truth shape your understanding of your need for prayer? In his model prayer, which we call the Lord's Prayer, what types of requests did Jesus include? In which of these areas might your own prayer life be lacking?

Lord, I want to be a person who prays powerfully, without ceasing. Help me pay attention to the Holy Spirit's promptings and respond prayerfully. In Jesus' name, amen.

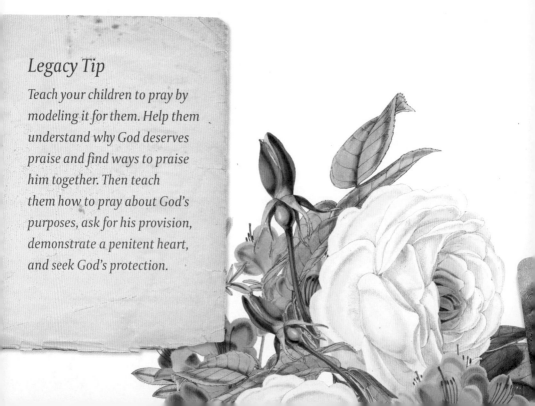

Legacy Tip

Teach your children to pray by modeling it for them. Help them understand why God deserves praise and find ways to praise him together. Then teach them how to pray about God's purposes, ask for his provision, demonstrate a penitent heart, and seek God's protection.

Genealogy Tip

USE WILLS TO ESTABLISH PARENT/CHILD RELATIONSHIPS

Do you need to firmly establish a parent/child relationship between ancestors? Search for a will. This type of probate record is the best tool to establish paternity and maternity. A will is a statement written by or on behalf of an individual who wished to pass down property, household goods, and other assets to his or her heirs. These documents include the names of heirs, names of executors, and instructions on how to carry out the will. After a person has died, the will is recorded at their local courthouse so the probate process can start.

17 The Beginning of a Legacy

If anyone is in Christ, the new creation has come: The old has gone, the new is here! All this is from God, who reconciled us to himself through Christ and gave us the ministry of reconciliation.

2 CORINTHIANS 5:17-18

A legacy must begin somewhere. Some families can trace their spiritual heritage back for centuries. Others witnessed the birth for themselves.

Jessica was just a toddler when Jesus forever changed her parents' lives. Their transformation highlights her earliest memories—a time of letting go of old things and learning how to walk with Jesus in a new life.

Growing up, Bob and Patty Thompson's lives were filled with alcohol, anger, and abuse—not a pretty legacy to bring into a new marriage, but it was all they'd ever known. Sadly, it shaped their new family as well.

For almost a decade, Bob and Patty led their family in the wrong direction. Each sought fun and fulfillment in partying, drinking, and other partners. Work-related stress and multiple miscarriages intensified the conflict at home, and the couple toyed with separation.

Then God began to soften Patty's heart. She knew her family needed a drastic change in order to survive, and she sensed they needed to move toward God. Patty began to attend church services and ask questions about God. She even took the entire family to a Billy Graham crusade, but the family remained adrift.

A spiritual turning point came for Patty after a "chance" meeting with a Christian woman named Barbara. This discerning woman sensed Patty's desperation and offered her friendship. At Barbara's church, Patty felt the Spirit's activity and heard God's truth. Patty's new hope encouraged Bob to accept an invitation to meet with the pastor, and he returned home a new man in Christ.

Bob and Patty joined a discipleship class for new Christians. They began taking their family to church and learned how to raise their children to love Jesus. Bob and Patty decisively turned their backs on their old way of life, which caused some of their family members and friends to turn their backs on them. Nevertheless, the couple remained firmly committed to following Jesus. Their faith forever changed their family's future; a new heritage of faith had begun.

READ 2 CORINTHIANS 5:14-19 AND REFLECT: When did your family's legacy of faith begin? Do you carry on this legacy with a saving, dynamic relationship with Jesus? Do you live for Christ or yourself? Are there things in your life you need to let go in order to model new life in Christ for your family?

> *Jesus, thank you for loving me, forgiving my sins, and making me a new spiritual creation! Continue to help me grow and bring that newness to full reality. Amen.*

Legacy Tip

Get rid of anything in your life you don't want to become a part of your family's spiritual heritage. Many bad habits—especially addictions—tend to trickle down to the next generation. Live today the way you want your children to live in the future. Get help if you need it.

Genealogy Tip

TAX LISTS PRE-1848

Before 1848, only men over the age of twenty-one appeared on the tax rolls. Women weren't listed because most were not allowed to own property at that time. A single woman's father controlled her possessions, and when she married, the ownership and rights to her possessions were transferred to her husband. In 1839, the tide began to change, starting in Mississippi, when it granted married women the right to own (but not control) property in their own names.[13] Other states followed, with different stipulations. In 1848, the state of New York passed the Married Women's Property Act, a law that became a template for other states to follow.[14]

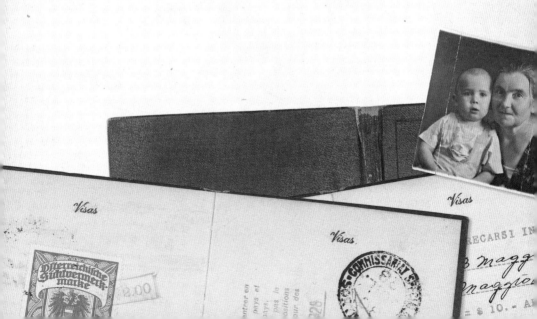

18 Dedicated to the Master

Whatever you do, in word or deed, do every-thing in the name of the Lord Jesus, giving thanks to God the Father through him.

COLOSSIANS 3:17, ESV

He may be the most famous artist you've never heard of. The master craftsman Giuseppe Guarneri del Gesù ranks among history's greatest violin makers. Though the Stradivarius is more well known, many great virtuosos prefer the robust sound of a Guarnerius.

Giuseppe Guarneri was born into a family of violin makers in Cremona, Italy, in 1698. His grandfather, Andrea Guarneri, apprenticed alongside Stradivari under the master luthier Nicolò Amati. Although Giuseppe learned his craft from his family, he worked to develop his own unique style, creating instruments that are now worth millions of dollars for the common musicians of his day.

The instrument's powerful tone is not the only feature that makes a Guarnerius violin unique. In 1731, Giuseppe began inserting an emblem to identify his work. Although using labels with the name of the head of the household was the customary practice, Guarneri's label featured a monogram formed from three Greek letters. This *nomen sacrum* represented the phrase "Jesus, Savior of Men."

Giuseppe Guarneri committed both his life and his life's work to his Savior. He recognized that the Master he loved had blessed him with the talent and ability to create a masterpiece. The violin maker's decision to give God the glory earned him the nickname "del Gesù," which means "of Jesus." Yes, the man who dedicated his work to Jesus was himself fully dedicated to his Lord.

Giuseppe's desire to extol (or praise) God compelled his brother's descendant Joanne to devote everything she does to the Lord. Joanne, who inherited the family's love for music, plays both the viola and the guitar. Like "del Gesù," Joanne knows that God gifts each person uniquely and calls them to serve him with these gifts. God calls all his children—from master violin makers and church pianists to CEOs and homemakers—to be committed to bringing glory to the Master Craftsman by doing everything in the name of Jesus.

READ 1 PETER 4:10-11 AND REFLECT: What spiritual gifts, talents, and life experiences has God given you? In what ways can you use them to serve others and glorify God? How can you also glorify God in your daily work and routine tasks?

Thank you, Father, not only for the gifts you've given me but also the opportunities to bless others and glorify you as I use them. Help me to be a good steward. In Jesus' name, amen.

Legacy Tip

Spend some time brainstorming with your children. Help them recognize the gifts and talents God has given them. Talk with them about how God also wants to use their life experiences, education, and skills. Encourage them to consider ways they can use these gifts in a God-honoring way to bless others.

Genealogy Tip

SOUTHERN, EASTERN, AND CENTRAL-EUROPEAN IMMIGRANTS

Did your ancestors hail from Eastern or Southern Europe? Between 1880 and 1920, a wave of 20 million immigrants arrived in the United States from that area of the world.[15] Immigrants from Eastern Europe were primarily Jews fleeing religious persecution in their home countries. Many Southern Europeans came seeking economic opportunity. They hoped to make a better life for themselves and their families in America. Beyond passenger lists and naturalization records, the US Census is the easiest way to determine the country of origin for your immigrant ancestors.

19 The Family Tree

There were fourteen generations in all from Abraham to David, fourteen from David to the exile to Babylon, and fourteen from the exile to the Messiah.

MATTHEW 1:17

In ancient cultures, families regularly talked about their ancestors. Ancient Israelites in particular valued ancestry records. In early Israel, some genealogies were written, and others were transmitted orally.[16] They told family stories around the cooking fire, as they walked, as they worked, and as they rested. Reciting the genealogies in this way made them personal. The stories became part of the fabric of daily life.

Genealogies served useful purposes. For instance, linear genealogies established claims to power, such as the right to sit on a throne. After the Israelites returned from exile, these records were vital for qualifying who could serve as priests. In addition, they proved kinship or family relationships between individuals. These relationships determined important matters, such as marriage, inheritance, and social obligations. One prime biblical example is Naomi and her daughter-in-law Ruth. Naomi's ability to prove her kinship connection to Boaz changed their future (Ruth 4:1-12).

The Old Testament contains about twenty-five genealogical lists, in addition to other registers of individuals and families. The New Testament includes two separate accounts of Jesus' ancestry, one in Matthew and one in Luke. These genealogical records reveal important truths about Jesus. Matthew clearly shows that Jesus descended from David, fulfilling God's promise of an eternal King (Matthew 1:6). Gentile women like Rahab and Ruth (Matthew 1:5) grace Matthew's list, highlighting the all-inclusive nature of Jesus' salvation. On the other hand, Luke traces Jesus' line all the way back to Adam, connecting Jesus with the entire human race.

Genealogies are not dry lists, but exciting road maps. They record history, tell family stories, and memorialize abiding faith. Don't skip these rich treasures in the Bible, and take time to mine them from your own family history as well.

READ MATTHEW 1:1-17 AND REFLECT: As you read the record of Jesus' genealogy, take note of significant names and connections. Research any unfamiliar names and learn their stories. What do these people and their connection to Christ reveal about your Savior?

Father, thank you for the individual stories of my family that contribute to who I am today. Help me to live in such a way that my children and grandchildren are enriched by my story. In Jesus' name, amen.

Legacy Tip

Research the life stories of individuals on your ancestral tree to find evidence of faith and courage in your family. Share these stories with your children and talk about the ways they set a godly example. Start a tradition of passing down your important stories of family legacy.

Genealogy Tip

STATE AND LOCAL MILITIAS

The American colonies needed protection, and establishing a militia was the answer. The militia of the colonial era is roughly equal to today's National Guard. Those who served led a full civilian life, and they also participated in regular training and took up arms in times of need. The colonies required most able-bodied men to serve in their local militia. Typically, the militia excluded slaves and indentured servants except during times of crisis. Each member was required to provide his own weaponry and equipment. They also had to participate in regular musters, training sessions, arms inspections, and drills. If they failed to report for musters, they could be punished under local laws. Look for militia records at the state or local levels to see if any of your ancestors participated.

20 Ripples of Influence

Christ himself gave the apostles, the prophets, the evangelists, the pastors and teachers, to equip his people for works of service, so that the body of Christ may be built up.

EPHESIANS 4:11-12

When a pebble breaks the surface of a still pond, the water ripples out in ever-widening circles. The small impact of one stone initiates a beautiful chain of movement. Likewise, one person can influence many. Even minor actions can ripple across the years, through multiple lives, flowing through the generations and beyond.

Born in 1890, Henrietta Mears was raised in a godly home in Minnesota. Her parents, especially her mother, carefully nurtured young Henrietta's spiritual life with daily Bible reading, family prayer, and hymns.[17] She gave her life to Christ at the age of seven and surrendered to full-time ministry at seventeen.

When she graduated from college, Henrietta taught high school chemistry and devoted endless hours to church lay leadership. In 1928, she accepted a call to be the director of Christian education at the First Presbyterian Church of Hollywood, where she led the Sunday school department and taught college-aged students. Under her leadership, Sunday school attendance jumped from 450 to more than 4,000 in just two and a half years.[18]

Henrietta's ministry shaped contemporary Bible study and discipleship. In 1933, she started Gospel Light Press and became the first publisher of Sunday school curriculum geared to specific grade levels. She taught churches how to train their leaders and cofounded the National Sunday School Association.

Her efforts to revitalize Christian education in churches across America paid off. Henrietta mentored countless young believers who made significant contributions to Christianity, including the founders of Campus Crusade for Christ, Young Life, and the Navigators. Future United States president Ronald Reagan sat under her discipleship.[19] And, most significantly, God used Henrietta and her ministry to encourage a young Billy Graham during a crisis of faith.[20]

God called Henrietta Mears to be an equipper, and the ripple effects of her faithful obedience are still evident today.

READ EPHESIANS 4:11-16 AND REFLECT: Are you taking an active role in your children's or grandchildren's spiritual growth? In what ways are they growing spiritually? Keeping their age in mind, evaluate their spiritual health and consider intentional ways to cultivate their growth.

Lord, thank you for the educational ministry of the church. Continue to provide equippers and teachers to build up and encourage your people. And, Father, give my family members a desire to know you more and to look more like Jesus. In his name, amen.

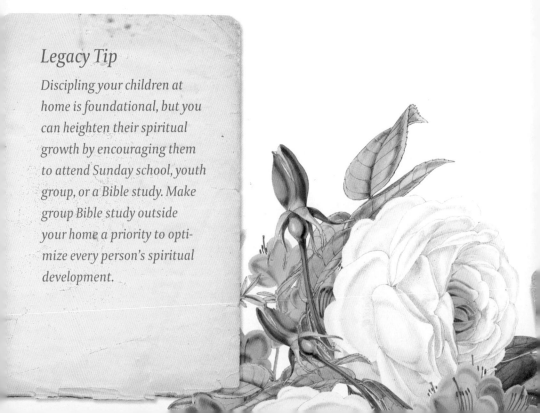

Legacy Tip

Discipling your children at home is foundational, but you can heighten their spiritual growth by encouraging them to attend Sunday school, youth group, or a Bible study. Make group Bible study outside your home a priority to optimize every person's spiritual development.

Genealogy Tip

PROBATE RECORDS

Death leaves a paper trail. Probate is the legal process that follows a person's passing. This process produces legal documents and probate records dealing with the individual's will and disposition of his or her property and assets. Since most heirs of a deceased individual are close relatives, probate records can reveal or prove family connections. The main types of probate records include wills, administrations, deeds of sale, deeds of gifts, guardianships, and estate distributions. In addition, there are a host of land records, including deeds, deeds of sale, deeds of gift, quitclaim deeds, surveys, land plats, and land warrants. These types of records can generally be found at the state and local levels.

21 A Grace-Filled Moment by the Rocker

I will open my mouth with a parable; I will utter hidden things, things from of old— things we have heard and known, things our ancestors have told us.

PSALM 78:2-3

An old rocking chair occupies a prominent place in Margaret's living room. Each time Margaret sits and rocks, she recalls sweet memories of her great-grandmother's stories, her vibrant faith, and God's abundant grace. Now, many decades after hearing those stories, Margaret is faithful to pass them on to her children and grandchildren.

Margaret's great-grandmother, Isabell Fleming, was born in 1883 in De Soto, Missouri. In her early teens, Isabell married William Fisher. William, desiring to help others both physically and spiritually, became a rural doctor and circuit preacher, traveling throughout Missouri, Arkansas, and Oklahoma. Isabell worked as his nurse and midwife and made many of the medicines they used. In the early 1900s, the family moved to Indian Creek, Arkansas, where they raised two sons and a daughter named Lenora. Lenora became Margaret's maternal grandmother.

Due to the geographical distance between them and some difficult family circumstances, Margaret didn't meet her great-grandmother Isabell until she was twelve. But it didn't take long for the two to develop a special bond. Margaret spent almost every Saturday with "Ma." During the summer, when school was out, Margaret and Ma had even more time together.

They enjoyed hours outside on the porch, with Ma in her rocker and Margaret close by. Ma taught Margaret how to sew and crochet. She told her about God and his great love for her. Although Ma's poor eyesight prevented her from reading her Bible to Margaret, she could still share the stories because she knew many of them by heart. Ma included such vivid details in her storytelling that Margaret could picture the crowd on the hillside listening to the Sermon on the Mount. She could hear Peter's bold testimony given to the multitude that gathered when the Holy Spirit arrived with power. And one grace-filled day, Margaret knelt beside Ma's rocker and, like the thousands on the Day of Pentecost, gave her life to Jesus.

"Ma" Isabell obeyed God's call to instill a legacy of faith in future generations. She told her great-granddaughter about God's mighty works and his commands. She gently guided Margaret to faith in Christ. And her influence laid the foundation of faith that would later lead Margaret into children's ministry. Every time Margaret shares a story about Jesus with a group of children, she thinks of Ma and the stories of old told from the rocker.

READ PSALM 78:1-8 AND REFLECT: Based on these verses, what is God's design for establishing a spiritual heritage? What should we tell our children and why? If you fail to tell your children and grandchildren about God, what might happen?

Father, I want to obey your command to tell future generations about you and your mighty works. Give me wisdom and insight to know how best to accomplish that. In Jesus' name, amen.

Legacy Tip

Obey God's command to teach your children about him. Find or develop a systematic plan to teach God's Word to them. Make use of casual moments and bedtimes, as well as intentional times of family devotions or Bible study. Help them understand how to apply what they learn to their lives.

Genealogy Tip

DONATE FAMILY HEIRLOOMS FOR SAFEKEEPING

Are you worried about the long-term protection of a family heirloom? Your full family story relies on the safety of irreplaceable possessions. Sometimes donating a historically valuable item is better than passing it down to an heir who can't protect it from damage. I know of one family's eighteenth-century Bible that was stored in an outdoor shed. The poor conditions ruined the heirloom and its usefulness to future genealogists. Before donating family heirlooms to a library, museum, or historical so-ciety, confirm that the depository is well-funded and willing to archive the item. Libraries, which receive government funding, most often have the resources needed to care for your heirloom. Historical societies and small museums are funded by individual donations and grants, making them less stable choices for the long term.

22 | Trustworthy Witnesses

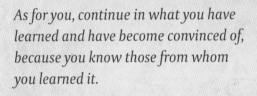

As for you, continue in what you have learned and have become convinced of, because you know those from whom you learned it.

2 TIMOTHY 3:14

One simple life lived by simply trusting God leaves a significant impact on everyone who watches. James Baker trusted the Lord, and his granddaughter Anisa trusted him. He was a reliable witness.

Anisa's grandpa lived his faith just like he breathed—naturally, consistently, and effortlessly. Grandpa Baker expressed his faith in God in unpretentious ways every day. He regularly mentioned the "good Lord" in his conversations as he recognized God's blessings. Grandpa also reflected God's love in all of his relationships by the way he treated everyone he encountered with love and kindness. He showed that his thoughts dwelled on eternity when he pointed to the sky and told Anisa about the mansions in heaven God had prepared for his children (John 14:2) and read the verse from the Bible that says Jesus is standing at the door of our hearts and knocking (Revelation 3:20).

God planted a seed of faith in Anisa's heart, and Grandpa Baker watered it. When Anisa sadly complained that she didn't have many friends, Grandpa said, "There's a friend in heaven you can always talk to." He also gave her a Bible storybook, and Anisa devoured every story. She believed the words were true, because she knew Grandpa got his wisdom from God's Word. Through his faithful witness, he introduced her to Jesus, who has become her greatest friend.

In the same way Anisa's faith was influenced by Grandpa Baker, Timothy's young faith was also encouraged to grow by people he trusted. As a child, Timothy first learned to trust God by watching his mother and grandmother consistently live out their faith (2 Timothy 1:5). When Timothy became a young man, the apostle Paul discipled and mentored him (2 Timothy 3:10). Timothy learned to trust what Paul taught him because, like Timothy's mother and grandmother, Paul never wavered.

He lived what he taught. Even when Paul faced persecution, he continued to proclaim Jesus' goodness and mercy.

Someone's testimony becomes trustworthy when others hear it displayed in their words and see it demonstrated through their actions. Timothy's mother and grandmother lived in ways that confirmed their testimony. Paul's life also confirmed his witness, and for that reason Timothy accepted what Paul taught. Grandpa Baker's life gave credibility to his testimony, so Anisa took to heart and valued his witness, which brought her closer to Jesus.

READ 2 TIMOTHY 3:10-17 AND REFLECT: When a person's actions don't align with their words, which do people usually believe? How did Paul confirm what he taught by the way he lived? Does the way you live fully match your words? Is there anything you need to realign?

Father, I am grateful to be one of your children, and my heart's desire is for my entire family to follow you. Help me not to be ashamed of the gospel and to boldly proclaim it to them. I want to be a consistent and trustworthy witness. In Jesus' name, amen.

Legacy Tip

Your actions make a deeper impact on your family than your words. Make sure your life consistently reflects what the Bible teaches about being a loyal follower of Jesus. When your life matches your words, others are more likely to listen to what you say. It won't take long for others to see how important Jesus is to you.

Genealogy Tip

VERIFY PUBLIC FAMILY TREES

Shortcuts are enticing because they seem like time-savers. Someone else has done the work, and it's all right there in black and white. If you are a member of a family tree website, it's tempting to pull data from other members' trees. Unfortunately, it's not uncommon for these online trees to contain errors. Before you accept their facts as your own and add them to your family tree, verify the research. Ensure that their sources are well-documented. Consider the information on these trees as "potential" facts, as possibilities to be verified.

God's greatness

PSALMS 96-99.

shew forth his salvation from day to day.
3 Declare his glory among the heathen, his wonders among all people.
4 For the LORD is great, and greatly to be praised: he is to be feared above all gods.
5 For all the gods of the nations are idols: but the LORD made the heavens.
6 Honour and majesty are before

11 Light is sown for the righteous, and gladness for the upright in heart.
12 Rejoice in the LORD, ye righteous; and give thanks at the remembrance of his holiness.

PSALM 98.
A Psalm.

O SING unto the

Exhortation to

PSALMS

PSALM 100.
A Psalm of praise.

MAKE a joyful noise unto the LORD, all ye lands.
2 Serve the LORD with gladness: come before his presence with

23 | A Faithful Founder

Since we are surrounded by such a great cloud of witnesses, let us throw off everything that hinders and the sin that so easily entangles. And let us run with perseverance the race marked out for us.

HEBREWS 12:1

Faithfulness. Endurance. Dedication. Service. These are just a few attributes that Virginia colonist Lieutenant Colonel Walter Chiles demonstrated.

Walter Chiles was born about 1609 in Bristol, England. Following in his father's footsteps, he became a textile merchant. He looked for a larger market in the American colonies around 1636, and two years later, he moved near Jamestown, Virginia, with his wife and two sons.[21]

That decision proved wise. Walter established and expanded his business, running merchant ships between America and places such as England and Holland. Walter also worked to protect and build up the community. He served in various political positions, including the Virginia House of Burgesses and the Virginia Governor's Council. And most important, Walter actively supported his faith community as an Anglican churchwarden.[22]

Walter laid a brick in the foundation of America. He set an example of hard work, service, and faith. He encouraged his community and his church to live peaceful, productive lives. And although he lived hundreds of years ago, Walter still serves as an example for his descendants today. Rebecca—one of the many Chiles cousins—follows in his footsteps by living in ways that honor God through service to her family and community. One of Becky's favorite ways to serve is by helping to meet the physical needs of the men at her local homeless veterans' shelter.

The author of Hebrews shows the benefit of knowing and following godly examples. In Hebrews 11, a chapter known as the "Hall of Faith," numerous heroes of the faith are highlighted. Through the centuries, these everyday men and women experienced difficulties and persevered, following God no matter the consequences. They are inspiring models to emulate as we continue to run the race God has set before us.

READ HEBREWS 12:1-3 AND REFLECT: In what ways do you exemplify faithfulness, endurance, and dedication to God to your family? What sin, habits, or hinderances do you need to lay down so you can freely and fully run a life of faith?

Father, thank you for the "great cloud of witnesses" who have gone before me. Help me to follow their examples by getting rid of anything in my life that prevents me from keeping my eyes on Jesus. In his name, amen.

Legacy Tip

Record your family's stories of faith and spiritual endurance for the generations that will come after you. It could be as simple as writing stories about yourself and your children in a journal. Or document your stories digitally, and when you have a large enough collection, have it printed or even self-published.

Genealogy Tip

BURNED RECORDS

Do you have colonial Virginians in your family tree? Researching ancestors who lived there can be tricky. A significant number of chancery
and judgment records from prior to 1860 are missing or no longer exist
because during the Civil War, Union forces burned multiple courthouses.
In one instance, thankfully, a local judge saved many volumes, including
deed books, will books, and order books, by removing them from the
courthouse for safekeeping before the devastation occurred. Other colonial records were lost due to natural disasters, the Revolutionary War, and
the War of 1812.[23]

24 | That They May Know Him

*Ask the Lord of the harvest, therefore,
to send out workers into his harvest field.*

MATTHEW 9:38

Twenty-nine years. That's how long Susan and her husband have been serving God as full-time missionaries. But Susan's passion for missions is a family legacy that began two generations earlier in the heart of her grandmother, Rose "Mimi" Fowler Maxwell.

Rose Maxwell was born in 1907 in Greenville, South Carolina. Her Christian parents helped her fall in love with Jesus. Soon Rose also fell in love with missions. She longed for people around the world to know her Lord. Rose served as the president of the Women's Missionary Union in her church, an organization that supports Southern Baptist missionaries around the world and educates the local church about missions.

Young Susan caught Mimi's enthusiasm for missions. Whenever missionaries visited her church, told their stories, and showed their slides, Susan was captivated. Even as a girl, Susan felt burdened for people around the world who needed to hear about Jesus.

Susan's parents fostered and encouraged her love for missions. When she was just seven, her father arranged a side trip during a family vacation to visit a Native American missionary in New Mexico whom Susan had written to as part of a church missions project. The missionary pastor gave Susan a piece of Native American pottery and a piece of petrified wood as reminders of his ministry.

Susan's mother intentionally involved her in local missions. Each week, she took Susan and a group of junior high girls from their church to work with children at a local housing project. For more than a year, Susan's mother and the girls did crafts, told Bible stories, shared the gospel, and showed the children Jesus' love.

When Susan was eight years old, Mimi suddenly passed away from a brain aneurysm. But her influence still lingers through her grand-daughter. Susan looks forward to the day when she will see Mimi again and recount her own God stories from the mission field. It will be a way to thank Mimi for the legacy she passed down.

READ MATTHEW 9:35-38 AND REFLECT: As a Christian, what responsibility do you have to spiritually lost people around the world? In what ways can you be involved in "bringing in the harvest"?

Father God, not everyone is called to be a missionary in a foreign country, but each of us is called to pray for those who haven't given their lives to you. Help me to find and support organizations that are spreading the gospel around the globe. In Jesus' name, amen.

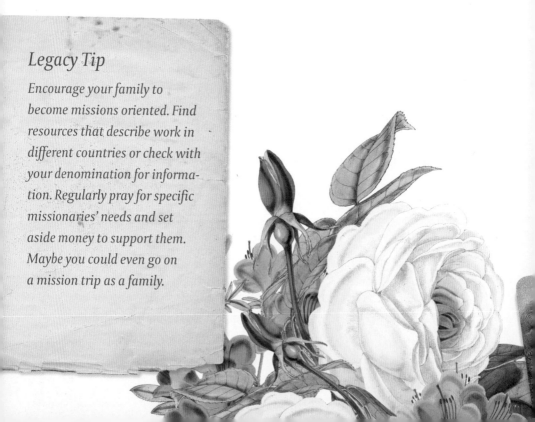

Legacy Tip

Encourage your family to become missions oriented. Find resources that describe work in different countries or check with your denomination for information. Regularly pray for specific missionaries' needs and set aside money to support them. Maybe you could even go on a mission trip as a family.

Genealogy Tip

ERRORS IN CENSUS REPORTS

It could be right, but it might be wrong. Census records are valuable research tools, but they're not always accurate. The massive undertaking of counting every citizen carries a lot of potential for mistakes. Census takers, or enumerators, visit every household in the community to collect the information and fill out the census forms. Many factors contribute to the level of accuracy. In the early decades of the US census, the poorly paid enumerators lacked proper supplies. They traveled long distances and worked long hours, enduring both mental and physical fatigue. Many enumerators lacked adequate education and struggled to communicate effectively with immigrant families. The families themselves also contributed to the inaccuracy. Some had trouble recalling the exact birth dates for various family members, while others reported nicknames rather than legal names.

25 The Desk

*"Bring the whole tithe into the storehouse, that there may be food in my house. Test me in this," says the L*ORD *Almighty, "and see if I will not throw open the floodgates of heaven and pour out so much blessing that there will not be room enough to store it."*

MALACHI 3:10

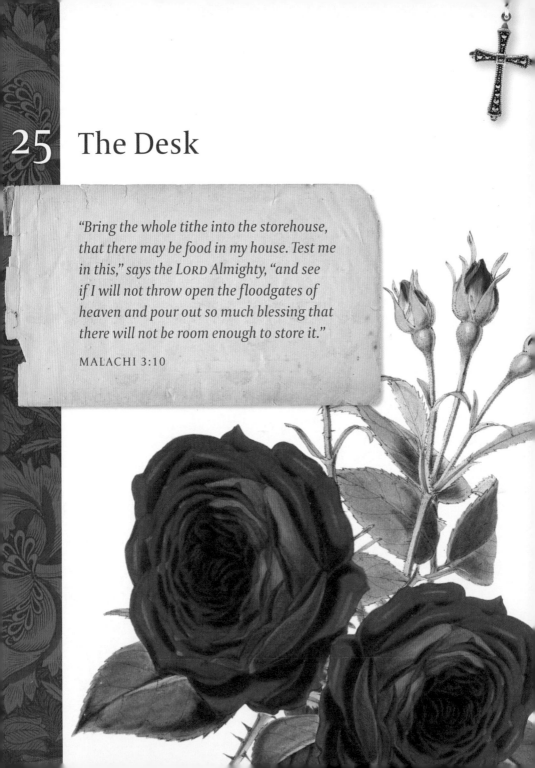

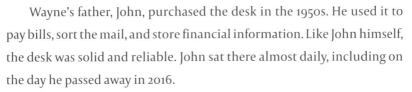

The small desk is plain and simple. Almost seven decades of use gently mark its wooden surface. A few tiny dings on the corners. A faint water ring on the top. Today, the desk stands under a sunny window in the guest bedroom of Wayne's home. A four-cup coffee pot and two blue mugs sit there on a tray, waiting for friends to visit. But the desk has seen busier times.

Wayne's father, John, purchased the desk in the 1950s. He used it to pay bills, sort the mail, and store financial information. Like John himself, the desk was solid and reliable. John sat there almost daily, including on the day he passed away in 2016.

For Wayne, the sturdy desk represents a strong spiritual truth, an unforgettable lesson his father faithfully exemplified. When Wayne was growing up, each Sunday morning he watched his father sit there and write his tithe check. Even if money was tight—and it often was—John wrote the check. He knew that everything he had belonged to God. John always trusted God, and God always proved trustworthy.

When Wayne graduated from high school, his older brother, Steve, graduated with his bachelor's degree from college. The family barely had enough money to help one son with college at a time. So when Steve was accepted to graduate school, his parents began to pray. Not much later, a forester contacted Wayne and Steve's mother. He wanted to buy timber from family land she had inherited, and it would provide enough to cover the extra expense for Steve's graduate tuition.

Wayne's parents tithed faithfully. They trusted God to always provide and to keep his promises. The desk reminds Wayne of the legacy of faith he has worked to pass down to his own children.

READ MALACHI 3:8-12 AND REFLECT: According to verse 8, who owns the money in your bank account? Does your view of your financial resources match the principles in this passage? What promise does God make? Do you trust God to provide? Have you ever "tested" his promise?

Lord, you are a faithful provider. Adjust my attitude about money. I know it all belongs to you, so guide me to use it wisely for your Kingdom. In Jesus' name, amen.

Legacy Tip

Be a good steward of all the resources God has given you. Make giving to God your first priority, and let your children know why you are committed to tithing. Show them that God is dependable and always supplies just what we need.

Genealogy Tip

STATE AND TERRITORIAL CENSUS REPORTS

If you can't find what you're looking for in the US census records, you may want to check the state or territorial census reports. Many marriages, births, deaths, and migrations happened during the ten years between each US census. Between the late eighteenth century and the early twentieth century, many individual states took their own censuses to bridge the gap. A state census can help you round out your research and provide a better picture of the ancestor you're tracing. Additionally, when a new US territory petitioned for statehood, it was required to take a territorial census to ensure they met the population requirements. Unfortunately, many territorial censuses are incomplete, and most are not indexed.

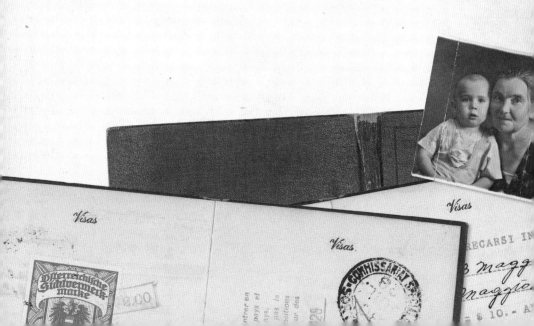

26 He Trusted the Promise Keeper

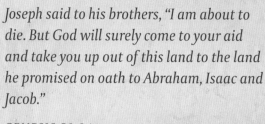

Joseph said to his brothers, "I am about to die. But God will surely come to your aid and take you up out of this land to the land he promised on oath to Abraham, Isaac and Jacob."

GENESIS 50:24

Joseph's life was marked by a series of mountains and valleys. After his brothers sold him to traders who were on their way to Egypt, he fell from favorite son to slave to prisoner, then rose from prisoner to second-in-command of Egypt. The power and prominence God gave him there provided the position Joseph needed to save his entire family from certain starvation in Canaan. Joseph was able to bring his father, his brothers, and their families to live with him in Egypt, where they survived an extended famine ravaging that entire region.

Although difficulty filled much of Joseph's life, he recognized God's hand in it all. Joseph acknowledged God's sovereignty in his circumstances, even his brothers' evil actions against him. After their father died, Joseph once again assured his brothers that he would not retaliate. "You intended to harm me, but God intended it for good to accomplish what is now being done, the saving of many lives" (Genesis 50:20).

Joseph also believed God would keep his promise to give a homeland to the descendants of his ancestors Abraham, Isaac, and Jacob. In fact, Joseph was so certain God would fulfill his promise that he instructed his family to carry his bones back with them when the time came. "By faith Joseph, when his end was near, spoke about the exodus of the Israelites from Egypt and gave instructions concerning the burial of his bones" (Hebrews 11:22).

God's purposes, plans, and promises are far greater than any individual. He executes them through the course of history. Great men and women of faith embrace this truth and help their children understand the vastness of God.

The Lord will keep his promises, but, like Joseph, we may not see all of them fulfilled in our lifetime. For instance, you may not live to see Jesus' promised return, and your children and grandchildren may not see it. Yet you can trust that he will come back. By grounding your life on the certainty of this promise, you will set an example of faith for your children.

READ GENESIS 50:22-26 AND REFLECT: How did Joseph's faith remain strong even in the face of death? Is your faith strong enough to enable you to trust in God's promises that are still unfulfilled? What are some ways you can build your faith in God as a Promise Keeper?

Father, thank you for your many promises. Help my trust in you as a Promise Keeper to grow stronger. Help me to set an example of trust for my family. In Jesus' name, amen.

Legacy Tip

Study God's promises that have not yet been fulfilled, such as Christ's return, the resurrection of Christians, and our eternal home with Jesus. Teach these promises to your children. Help them understand that even though they may not see them fulfilled in their lifetimes, God faithfully keeps his promises. Talk about how they should live in light of this certainty.

Genealogy Tip

ESTATE ADMINISTRATION ACCOUNTS

When someone dies, his or her assets, including property, cash, financial securities, and possessions, are known as the *estate*. *Estate administration* is the collection and management of these assets. Estate administration accounts often include an inventory of the property of the deceased individual, as well as information about the sale of property and a list of debts owed by the deceased. Administration records don't always include information about relationships, but they can be helpful in establishing residency and the date of the relative's death. *Intestate* means the individual did not have a will at the time of death. In this case, the courts divide and distribute the deceased's estate among the heirs.

27 A Small and Mighty Messenger

How beautiful on the mountains are the feet of the messenger who brings good news, the good news of peace and salvation, the news that the God of Israel reigns!

ISAIAH 52:7, NLT

Some people might have looked at Edith O'Connell and thought, *How sad.* Her humped and twisted back, the result of childhood polio, had compressed her torso and reduced her height significantly. Her feet were misshapen, but thankfully she could walk with special orthopedic shoes. Even so, she found it painful to stand for long periods. None of her other dozen siblings had contracted polio, which was a blessing for them. But where was the blessing for Edith?

In a small Baptist church, she heard how God loved her. He saw her heart, not her crippled body. She gave her life to Christ. When she invited her sisters to church, their lives changed too. But God had more plans for Edith.

She began teaching Sunday school. Being small had its advantages; the children loved that she was their size. Then Edith heard about an organization called Child Evangelism Fellowship (CEF). The ministry was a perfect fit, and soon Edith hosted her first Good News Club.

More than a dozen children sat on the grass in Edith's backyard facing a flannel board. As she told the Bible story, Edith placed depictions of people and key items on the board to help the children remember the details. Noah's ark and the animals, Jonah and the whale, Jesus on the cross and an empty tomb.

One regular attendee at that Saturday club was Edith's niece Bonne. When she was six years old, she prayed with Aunt Edith and asked Jesus into her heart. At summer's end, Edith continued her evangelistic outreach in a CEF trailer at the county fair. Bonne and her cousins went each day, inviting children to come inside the trailer to hear a wonderful story and receive a Wordless Book.[24]

As an adult, Bonne combined her love for God with her love of stories when she became a Christian magazine editor and book editor. She is able to help people tell how God has changed their lives. Aunt Edith brought the Bible to life for Bonne, and she in turn recounted those stories to family members—including her niece and nephew on long car rides and her great-niece Julia, who played Sunday school teacher and retold the stories to her granny in the living room. Powerful story threads were woven into a family's spiritual tapestry, and it all started when Edith passed on the Good News about Jesus to the children in her sphere of influence.

READ ISAIAH 52:7-10 AND REFLECT: What are the qualities of the Good News described in this passage? How would the people of Jerusalem respond to this news? Reflect on the truth that eternal salvation through Jesus Christ is the best news in human history, and commit to sharing this news with excitement and joy.

Lord Jesus, your gift of salvation is truly good news for all. Give me joy and excitement that are contagious as I share this news with those who desperately need to hear it. Amen.

Legacy Tip

God has given you a wide circle of influence—extended family members, friends, neighbors, and coworkers. Create opportunities to share the Good News with them. It can be as simple as including an evangelistic tract in your annual Christmas card or a bit more involved. Maybe you want to host a summer backyard Bible club at your home.

Genealogy Tip

PHOTOGRAPH IDENTIFICATION

Who's in that photo? Many old photographs have names written on the back. If the handwriting appears to be old, you can be confident that the person in the photo is actually who you think it is. The older the writing, the more likely that's the correct identity. But don't speculate if you aren't sure—an incorrect identification shared online can confuse, disappoint, and frustrate other researchers. Carefully preserve old photo treasures and prevent further fading. Protect them from light, humidity, and temperature change by storing them in archival-quality sleeves, albums, or boxes. If you want to display the photos, make copies of them to frame and enjoy while you safely store the originals.

28 The Grandmother Who Helped a Child See

*One generation commends your works
to another; they tell of your mighty acts.*

PSALM 145:4

She received invitations to meet with presidents and governors. She was the first woman to speak before the US Senate. During her lifetime, she authored more than eight thousand hymns, many of which are still sung in churches today—beloved songs such as "Blessed Assurance," "To God Be the Glory," and "Near the Cross." Yes, Fanny Crosby left an enduring legacy of faith. But it began with her grandmother.

Frances Jane Crosby was born to John and Mercy Crosby in 1820. Tragedy marked the first year of her life. She lost her sight when she was six weeks old, because an incompetent doctor mistreated a mild eye inflammation. The hot mustard poultice he applied to her young eyes left her completely blind. Not long before her first birthday, Fanny's father died. Mercy, forced to work as a maid to support the family, left Fanny in the daily care of her grandmother, Eunice Crosby.

Grandmother Eunice lovingly dedicated herself to be Fanny's "eyes." She took her granddaughter for long walks, helping her "see" what the two encountered through vivid descriptions. Eunice taught Fanny about colors, flowers, and birds. She painted glorious word pictures of sunrises and sunsets. Eunice also read constantly to Fanny, particularly from the Bible, and helped Fanny memorize many passages of Scripture.[25]

Fanny spent most of her young years with Eunice, and the two became very close. Later in life, in writing about her relationship with her grandmother, Fanny stated, "My grandmother was more to me than I can ever express by word or pen."[26]

In many ways, Eunice gave her granddaughter the world, challenging her not to allow blindness to be an excuse for not pursuing life to its fullest. More important, Eunice gave Fanny God's Word. The Lord's truths, firmly ingrained in her heart and mind, grew even stronger as she aged.

Years later, the truths flowed out as poetry, birthed to commend God's works to generations of believers.

READ PSALM 145:1-7 AND REFLECT: Praise must begin in our own hearts before we can tell future generations about God's mighty works. As you read this passage, note reasons to praise God. Then use these verses in a prayer, declaring his great deeds and meditating on his holiness.

> *Lord God, you are great and deserving of all praise! Your works are mighty, and I will declare them to each member of my family. Help all of us to see the good things you do in our lives. In Jesus' name, amen!*

Legacy Tip

Help inspire your family to recognize God's majesty. Perhaps you can take a nature walk together. Along the way, stop and pray, praising God for his attention to details, the vast breathtaking beauty of his creation, and the evidence of his creativity all around you. Or sing one of Fanny Crosby's hymns during your family devotional time.

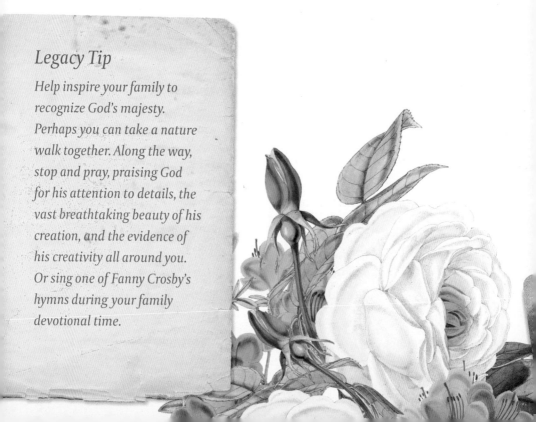

Genealogy Tip

BOUNTY LAND

Land is a great incentive. Between 1788 and 1855, the federal government offered land to entice men to enlist in the military. Congress awarded bounty-land warrants to veterans who served in the Revolutionary War, the War of 1812, the Mexican War, and a variety of Indian wars. Bounty-land warrants were certificates given to eligible veterans that granted them the right to free land in the public domain. These bounty-land warrants could be passed to a veteran's heir. Look for bounty-land records in the National Archives and Records Administration (NARA). They may contain valuable genealogical information. If you cannot locate a bounty-land or pension record in the National Archives, research local court records.[27]

29 | Standing with God

> *The community is to have the same rules for you and for the foreigner residing among you; this is a lasting ordinance for the generations to come. You and the foreigner shall be the same before the LORD.*
>
> NUMBERS 15:15

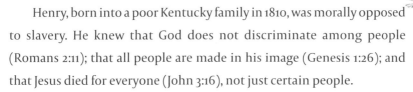

Before the Civil War, much of the American South made its living on the backs of slaves. Many slave owners often used God's Word to rationalize this wicked practice and protect their healthy bank accounts. Many people in the South accepted this cruel institution to maintain their status in the community. But not coal miner Henry Harris.

Henry, born into a poor Kentucky family in 1810, was morally opposed to slavery. He knew that God does not discriminate among people (Romans 2:11); that all people are made in his image (Genesis 1:26); and that Jesus died for everyone (John 3:16), not just certain people.

Prejudice is nothing new. Ancient male Jews, believing they were superior, regularly thanked God that they weren't female or Gentile. In Galatians, Paul wrote to correct this kind of discriminatory thinking. Our attitude should always align with God's, even when it goes against the cultural tide.

When Henry married the daughter of a well-to-do Tennessee plantation owner with more than twenty slaves, he still didn't waver in his determination to stand with God. People scorned and ridiculed Henry for his countercultural beliefs. His community labeled him as "white trash." But Henry's conviction remained firm, and he continued to side with God.

As he raised his family, Henry instilled in his children biblical truths about the evils of slavery. When Henry's son William married, a friend gave him three slaves as a wedding gift. Like his father, William believed God looked on all people as equal, so he refused the gift. And like his father, William was disdained for doing the right thing.

This legacy of truth and equality passed through the generations to Henry's great-great-grandson Tom, who is thankful for his ancestors' examples. "They sacrificed their social and economic status to what was right." That's a legacy to celebrate.

READ GALATIANS 3:26-29 AND REFLECT: How does God feel about different types of people? What breaks down the barriers that people so often build? Identify any patterns of thinking or attitudes in yourself and in your family that don't align with God's ways.

Father, strip away every ounce of bigotry and prejudice that is ingrained in my heart and mind. Help me to see people as you see them—individuals you have created and love and for whom your Son died. Align my heart with yours. In Jesus' name, amen.

Legacy Tip

Model a godly attitude before your family regarding people of different races, socioeconomic standings, cultures, religions, and political views. Teach them what the Bible says about the value of all people, especially God's love for them.

Genealogy Tip

VALIDATE DATES OF LIFE EVENTS

You've spent many hours and significant brain power researching and interpreting your family tree. But do the time lines make sense? Or is there confusion and contradiction? You can clear things up by validating the dates of significant life events. One effective way to corroborate your research is to compare dates between multiple generations. Check things like marriage, birth, and death dates, as well as immigration data. If you find conflict or contradiction, take a closer look. Analyzing the dates, places, and relationships will help you determine the accuracy of your research.

30 Open Kitchen, Open Heart

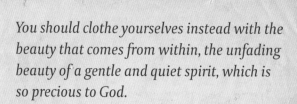

You should clothe yourselves instead with the beauty that comes from within, the unfading beauty of a gentle and quiet spirit, which is so precious to God.

1 PETER 3:4, NLT

Lisa has a fitting description of her paternal grandmother, Goldie Pepper Worthey: "Her Bible was always open, and her kitchen was never closed." Goldie faithfully followed God and humbly served others from her home for more than seven decades.

Growing up in northern Alabama, Lisa lived just one county away from Goldie. Each Sunday after church, her family took two-lane country roads to Goldie's house and spent the afternoon. As soon as she was tall enough to see over the edge of the counter, Lisa began working with Goldie in the kitchen. Her favorite job was to check the cornbread to see if the cornmeal mixture had softened enough to go in the oven.

Lisa loved their special time together. Her grandmother's gentle spirit and joyful contentment filled the small space and settled on Lisa like a warm blanket. The hours and days spent with Goldie planted a desire in her heart to serve others as her grandmother did.

Goldie mentored Lisa through quiet conversations and a consistent example of humility. While her beloved husband operated the general store that served Capshaw, Alabama, Goldie worked tirelessly in and around the house. Her large, carefully tended garden produced an abundance of corn, lima beans, and peas—much of which went into the freezer. In the fall, a variety of apples weighed down the branches of the trees around the edge of her garden. When the fruit was harvested, Goldie dried apple slices on the tin roof of the smokehouse. And she was generous with all of it.

These homegrown resources were Goldie's ministry tools. She eagerly opened her home to guests and always responded to illness and loss in the community by providing kindness and delicious food. Goldie lived a life of devoted service to others. In 1989, when she passed away at the age of ninety-two, the whole community grieved. Through the years, nearly everyone had enjoyed a gift from her kitchen and each one had received her love.

Goldie lived what the Bible teaches. Her home was a place of ministry. And she taught her granddaughter to use the simple, ancient tasks of home life to encourage, comfort, and support others. Today, Lisa's kitchen is a ministry hub just like her grandmother's. It's the gathering place for family and friends, and each guest is welcomed and loved. Lisa intentionally plans menus and snacks that will please others and make them feel special. And like Goldie, she never lets guests leave empty-handed.

READ TITUS 2:3-5 AND REFLECT: Is your home a place of ministry or seclusion? What resources has God given you that you can use to comfort and encourage others who come to your home?

Legacy Tip

Hospitality is different from entertaining. Entertaining focuses on the host and the house. Hospitality focuses on simply making the guest feel welcome. A comfortable place to sit, simple food, and warm, encouraging conversation is really all you need. Make the time to teach your children the basic tasks they will need to use their homes as hubs for ministry.

Father, I am delighted to have people in my home. Thank you for assuring me that ministering to others through hospitality doesn't need to be elaborate—it can be as simple as offering them a cup of coffee and a cookie. Open my eyes to the opportunities you give me to encourage others. In Jesus' name, amen.

Genealogy Tip

WORKING CLASS BRITISH ANCESTORS

Are there some blue-collared Brits on your family tree? The Industrial Revolution began in Great Britain in the latter half of the eighteenth century. Mechanized production created a massive need for workers in mills and factories. If you have ancestors who lived in Great Britain during that time, you may be able to find information about them online. Search for databases that are sources of historical information on industry and manufacturing during the late 1700s through the early 1800s. You may be able to find an ancestor on an employee roster for one of the many mills and factories that existed in the UK during this time period.

God's greatness

PSALMS 96–99.

shew forth his salvation from day to day.

3 Declare his glory among the heathen, his wonders among all people.

4 For the LORD *is* great, and greatly to be praised: he *is* to be feared above all gods.

5 For all the gods of the nations *are* idols: but the LORD made the heavens.

6 Honour and majesty

11 Light is sown for the righteous, and gladness for the upright in heart.

12 Rejoice in the LORD, ye righteous; and give thanks at the remembrance of his holiness.

PSALM 96

A Psalm.

O SING unto the

Exhortation to

PSALM

PSALM 100.

A Psalm of praise.

MAKE a joyful noise unto the LORD, all ye lands.

2 Serve the LORD with gladness: come before his presence with

31 | Sowing the Word

The rain and snow come down from the heavens and stay on the ground to water the earth. They cause the grain to grow, producing seed for the farmer and bread for the hungry. It is the same with my word. I send it out, and it always produces fruit. It will accomplish all I want it to, and it will prosper everywhere I send it.

ISAIAH 55:10-11, NLT

Just before the outbreak of World War I, Peter Zine fled what had been Ukraine with nothing but the clothes on his back. Eventually making his way to Connecticut, Peter met a young Ukrainian woman named Julia. They fell in love, married, and settled into a humble home in a small Ukrainian neighborhood in East Hartford. The garden and chicken coop in the backyard provided much of the family's food. It was a simple but happy life.

Then the stock market crashed in 1929, ushering in the most severe economic downturn the industrialized world has ever experienced. During America's Great Depression, millions lost jobs, homes, and farms. In desperation, able-bodied men took to the roads, rails, and rivers, moving from one town to the next in search of any available work.

Many of these traveling, hardworking hobos passed by the Zines' home, which was close to the Connecticut River. The Zines didn't have much food to spare, but when individuals knocked on the door begging for something to eat, they were never turned away. Peter gave them a bowl of oatmeal and sat with them on the back porch.

The oatmeal temporarily satisfied the hobos' hunger, but Peter knew their spiritual hunger was far greater. While they ate, Peter read Scriptures about Jesus and his sacrifice on the cross. Though Peter was not a preacher, nor was he especially eloquent, he knew the saving power of God's Word.

Peter's faithfulness to share also planted a seed in the heart of his granddaughter Julie. That seed took root and grew. Now Julie sows God's Word through a writing and teaching ministry. And she often wonders about the seeds her grandfather sowed. Perhaps some sprouted in the hearts of a few hobos.

READ ISAIAH 55:6-11 AND REFLECT: According to verse 7, what great spiritual need does mankind have? Contemplate the power of God's Word to meet that need. How should God's promise in verse 11 encourage us to share his Word with others?

Savior, make me and my family unashamed of the gospel. Give us a desire to tell people about what you did for everyone in the world. Bring to mind our family members who need you, and help us seize opportunities to tell others about you. Amen.

Legacy Tip

Equip your children to be evangelists. Talk about why salvation is necessary and how God provides it through Jesus. Teach them how to share the Good News of God's salvation with others. Help them memorize or mark key verses in their Bibles and practice telling their own salvation story aloud to you.

Genealogy Tip

MORTALITY SCHEDULES

In four United States censuses, enumerators also asked families about who had died in the previous twelve months. The government used these answers to produce the mortality schedule, another type of federal census schedule. These documents can prove the age of an ancestor who died in the year before the federal count. Mortality schedules may give an individual's place of birth, month and year of death, and age at death. Though these schedules are not available for all communities, they are available for the 1850 through 1880 federal census years and for six state censuses taken in 1885.

The Mother Behind the Brothers

She opens her mouth with wisdom, and the teaching of kindness is on her tongue.

PROVERBS 31:26, ESV

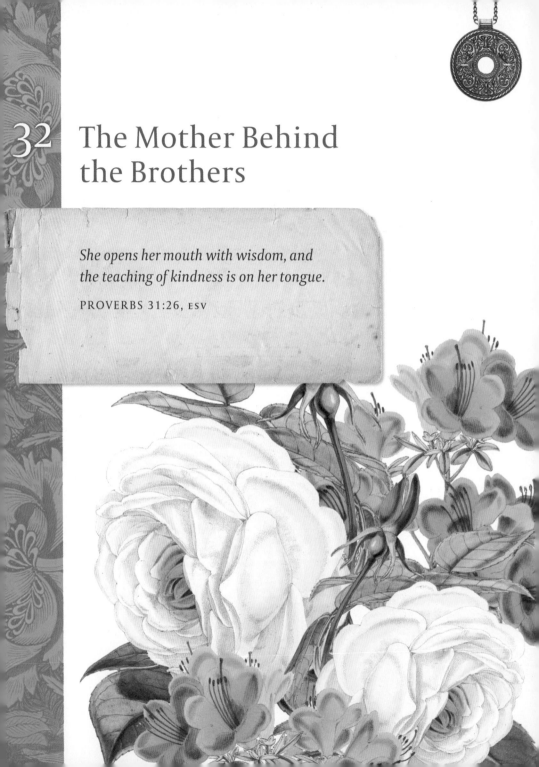

In the first half of the eighteenth century, John Wesley helped spark a spiritual revival in England that spread all the way to America. His ministry began an evangelical movement that would later become the Methodist Church. John's younger brother, Charles, also made a lasting contribution to the church. He composed thousands of hymns for worship, many of which are still sung today.

The significant impact of the Wesley brothers can be traced back to their mother, Susanna, who laid the solid foundation of faith in their lives. Historians largely credit the Wesleys' tremendous spiritual leadership to Susanna's influence and prayers.[28]

Born in 1669, Susanna Annesley Wesley was a minister's daughter and the youngest of twenty-five children. At age twenty, she married Samuel Wesley, a minister in the Church of England. Their marriage was rocky and marked by loss. Only half of their nineteen children survived to adulthood. Due to his excessive spending, Samuel spent time in debtor's prison. The family lost their home in a fire. And an argument initiated a marital separation of several months.[29]

Through all the turmoil and grief, Susanna was an unwavering constant in the lives of her children. She found her strength in God, spending an hour each day in prayer and Bible study. She committed six hours, six days a week, to the academic and spiritual education of her children. In addition, Susanna purposefully set aside an hour per week with each child to talk about spiritual things.[30]

Susanna discipled her children her entire life. She wrote encouraging letters to her sons and challenged them to remain fervent in their walk with God, and she compiled Christian education materials for her daughters. And, as only God can do, through her children he exponentially multiplied her efforts to benefit countless others.

READ PROVERBS 31:10-31 AND REFLECT: What characteristics do you see in the Proverbs 31 woman that make her helpful to her family? How does her life glorify God? Which of these characteristics do you already reflect? Which would you like to develop to benefit your family?

Lord God, I am inspired by mothers who realize how vital their children's spiritual condition is to their overall well-being. Give me insight on ways I can spiritually nurture and embolden each one of mine. In Jesus' name, amen.

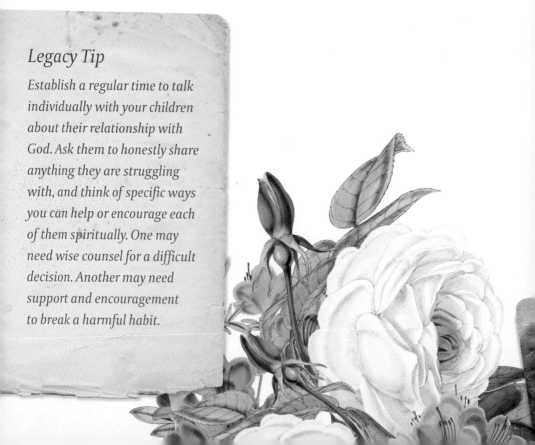

Legacy Tip

Establish a regular time to talk individually with your children about their relationship with God. Ask them to honestly share anything they are struggling with, and think of specific ways you can help or encourage each of them spiritually. One may need wise counsel for a difficult decision. Another may need support and encouragement to break a harmful habit.

Genealogy Tip

FAMILY CEMETERIES ON PRIVATE PROPERTY

Do you want to visit an ancestor's grave? Many of your ancestors may be buried in a family cemetery on private property. The codes vary from state to state, so research your state's laws before entering private property to visit a family cemetery. Landowners and lessees in some states are obligated to allow family members access to their ancestors' burial sites, but it isn't wise—or polite—to show up unannounced. Head off any potential problems by contacting the landowners ahead of time to get permission to enter their property. Give them a date and time when you plan to visit.

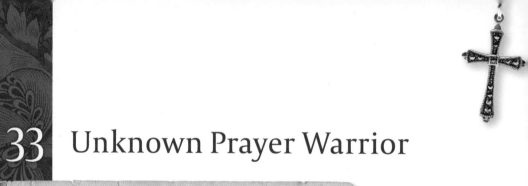

33 | Unknown Prayer Warrior

She lived as a widow to the age of eighty-four. She never left the Temple but stayed there day and night, worshiping God with fasting and prayer.

LUKE 2:37, NLT

For decades, Mrs. Coleman fought for Kim—battling daily on her knees. The carpet was worn where she knelt, regularly petitioning her heavenly Father on Kim's behalf, though at the time Kim didn't know it.

When Kim and her pastor husband, Barri, moved back to her hometown and bought a house in the same neighborhood where she had grown up, Kim recognized the house across the street.

"My siblings and I went to a backyard Bible club there every summer," she told her husband. "Mrs. Coleman was our teacher. I wonder if she still lives there."

As Kim stood at the front door of her neighbor's house, memories of the Bible club from twenty years before came flooding back. *If Mrs. Coleman answers the door, will she remember me?*

The door opened, and there she stood. When Kim introduced herself, Mrs. Coleman smiled, took her hand, and asked about Kim's siblings by name. "Please come in, Kim."

After visiting for a while, Mrs. Coleman pulled out a well-worn notebook. The red cover had faded with age and the pages were frayed. On each page Mrs. Coleman had written the names of the children who had attended the backyard Bible club. But that wasn't all she had recorded there. More important, the notebook documented the lengthy history of Mrs. Coleman's prayers. Every day, she prayed for the kids who came to Bible club. Every day, by name, for decades.

Over the years some of the now-grown kids had stopped by to see her. Whenever they did, Mrs. Coleman updated their information in her notebook and asked how she could continue to pray for them. "What about you, Kim? Anything I can take to the Lord for you?"

God alone knows the full impact Mrs. Coleman's prayers made on the many lives she influenced. The children didn't know she prayed for them, but this unknown prayer warrior never quit.

The prophetess Anna also did battle on her knees. For decades, she faithfully prayed for the fulfillment of God's promises. For decades she expectedly watched for his answer. Then one day, the Promised One entered the Temple and Anna's petition turned to praise.

READ LUKE 2:22, 36-38 AND REFLECT: What does verse 37 reveal about Anna's devotional life and relationship to God? Can you think of ways to remind yourself to pray specifically for your family more often? Do you remember to thank God for answered prayer?

Father, show me how to be a faithful prayer warrior. Give me wisdom and discernment to know how best to pray for each person in my family. Give me energy to keep praying and not give up. In Jesus' name, amen.

Legacy Tip

Keep a journal to record prayers for individual family members. Include dates and how God answers. Periodically show—or even give—these journals to them to encourage them to stay on God's path. When you fill one journal, start a new one.

Genealogy Tip

WHAT IS A GEDCOM?

Do you want to share your genealogical findings? Consider using GEDCOM. This acronym stands for Genealogical Data Communication. GEDCOM is a universally accepted file format that allows researchers to upload family trees from different applications. For instance, if you are a member of Ancestry.com, you can share your data with your cousin who uses Family Tree Maker, exporting your family tree, photos, and records so they synchronize with his or her data. A GEDCOM file is plain text that contains genealogical information about an individual, and it enables genealogists to upload, store, and exchange all kinds of genealogical information.

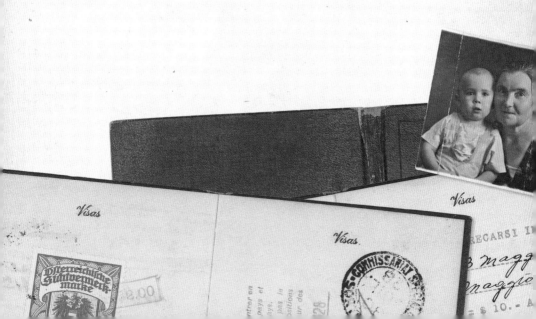

34 | Stop Asking and Start Believing

All your words are true; all your righteous laws are eternal.

PSALM 119:160

The shiny black Mary Janes pinched her toes, and the dainty white socks trimmed with lace crept down past her ankles and balled up under the arches of her small feet. But something else had captured the attention of six-year-old Deborah.

In the summer of 1958, Deborah's annual visit to her grandmother's home in Appomattox County, Virginia, always coincided with Granny's church's yearly revival. Three nights in a row, Deborah and her grandmother Annie McCormick went to church. Three nights in a row, they heard a message from God's Word. Three nights in a row, the preacher gave an invitation to respond to the Lord. And all three nights, while the pianist played "Just As I Am," young Deborah stepped into the aisle and answered the call.

She hadn't been able to resist. She knew all the Bible stories. She knew she loved Jesus. But each night, the music stirred a deep desire in her heart. The melody compelled Deborah to walk down the aisle and tell the preacher she wanted to give her life to Jesus. On the fourth night of the revival, after the congregation sang all five verses of "Just As I Am," and finally with every head bowed and every eye closed, Deborah once again felt the overwhelming need to respond. But as she stepped toward the aisle, Granny caught the hem of her dress. Bending close to Deborah's ear, she whispered, "There comes a time when you have to stop asking and start believing."

Granny taught Deborah a valuable lesson that night. God's Word is always true. Whether it's trusting his gift of salvation or believing his many promises, hearing God's truth is just the beginning. To this day, Deborah believes it, trusts it, and lives by it. And just like Granny, when Deborah's family needs a little encouragement to trust God's Word, she says, "Stop asking and start believing."

READ PSALM 119:89-93 AND REFLECT: What do these verses teach you about the nature of God and his Word? How should these truths impact the way you live every day? Thank God for the glorious truth that he is eternally faithful to uphold his Word.

Father, I believe that your Word is true and you are always faithful to keep it. Thank you that I can always trust you. In Jesus' name, amen.

Legacy Tip

Give your child, grandchild, niece, or nephew a Bible with your favorite promises of God highlighted. Add a brief note to a page in the front or back of the Bible detailing ways God fulfilled those promises in your life. Read these promises together and talk about God's faithfulness to always keep his word.

Genealogy Tip

UNDERREPRESENTED ANCESTORS

Are you having trouble finding certain ancestors in the US census? Census rolls can sometimes be unreliable, particularly for certain segments of the population. In times past, women, minorities, immigrants, and young children were often underrepresented on the census reports and tax lists. Don't depend on the census if you are searching for someone who falls into one of these categories. Instead, search in church records. Churches kept records long before the government began, and they could be the key to finding information about an ancestor's place of worship, maiden name, date of birth, and place of birth.

35 She Inspired a Movement

> *There was in Joppa a disciple named Tabitha, which, translated, means Dorcas. She was full of good works and acts of charity.*
>
> ACTS 9:36, ESV

Dorcas belongs to a very exclusive club. She and her fellow "resuscitation club" members, including Lazarus and Jairus's daughter, were restored to life after experiencing physical death. Dorcas was a follower of Christ in the first century, and she was known for her kindness and generosity. For her, charitable acts were not obligations—they were a way of life. Dorcas devoted her time, talents, and resources to help those in need.

And then the unthinkable happened: This servant-hearted woman fell ill and died. The local believers knew the apostle Peter was just eleven miles away in Lydda, so two men hurried to find him. Within a matter of hours, Peter arrived. The mourners surrounding Dorcas's body held up the garments she had made for them, a visual and moving testimony to her selfless life. She had helped these widows, and when she died, they felt her loss keenly.

After asking everyone to leave the room, Peter knelt and prayed, petitioning God on behalf of the widows. They not only *needed* Dorcas—they *loved* this precious servant of Christ. God miraculously answered Peter's prayer and brought Dorcas back to life. Imagine the joy of these believers when Peter presented her alive and well to them.

Dorcas's restoration not only encouraged the believers in Joppa, it also added to their number. Many who heard about the miracle "believed in the Lord" (Acts 9:42). Yes, God worked through Dorcas's life to help those in physical need. But he worked through her death to help those in spiritual need.

Dorcas's story is recounted with just a few verses, but her legacy inspired a movement of Christian women who followed her example of mercy and generosity. Charitable sewing groups have formed all across the globe, and many of them are called "Dorcas circles."

READ ACTS 9:36-42 AND REFLECT: How did Dorcas respond to the needs around her? How do you think the widows felt when Dorcas was restored to them? How can you help others right around you? What can you provide to improve their circumstances?

Father, open my eyes to specific conditions in my church and community. Show our family how we can help meet those needs as well as encourage others to join us. In Jesus' name, amen.

Legacy Tip

As a family, identify some physical needs in your community. Brainstorm ways you could meet one or more of them together. Prayerfully decide where to start, then act. For instance, you might volunteer at a local soup kitchen or food pantry, adopt a needy family for Christmas, or shovel snow or do yard work for an elderly neighbor.

Genealogy Tip

NATIVE AMERICANS AND THE CENSUS

Finding your Native American ancestors in the US census records may not be simple. Before 1900, the federal census taken every ten years included only a few of them, and none of the censuses prior to 1840 counted them at all. The 1860 census identified Native Americans living among the general population. In 1880, a special census recorded the names of Native Americans who did not appear on tax rolls. This report included individuals living on reservations and in unsettled areas of the country such as Washington Territory, Dakota Territory, and California. Beginning with the 1900 census, enumerators added Native Americans both living on reservations and in the general population to their total counts.

36 | From Horseback to Podcasts

How then will they call on him in whom they have not believed? And how are they to believe in him of whom they have never heard? And how are they to hear without someone preaching? And how are they to preach unless they are sent?

ROMANS 10:14-15, ESV

"**N**either snow nor rain nor heat nor gloom of night stays these couriers from the swift completion of their appointed rounds." Sound familiar? This description, borrowed from similar words written by Herodotus about mounted Persian postal couriers in the fifth century BC, can be seen above the entrance to the New York City Post Office on 8th Avenue.[31] This tribute to American postal workers could also be used to describe the nineteenth-century itinerant evangelist Thomas Melton.

Born in 1853, Thomas Ely Melton was a circuit preacher and tent revival evangelist. Traveling on horseback from church to church throughout West Virginia, Thomas relied on God's provision and the kind hospitality of others for housing and physical needs. He was fully committed to his calling, determined to overcome any and every obstacle. He refused to allow inclement weather to hinder his God-given work. Sometimes when he returned home late on frigid nights, family members would have to chip away the ice that encased his boots in the saddle stirrups before he could dismount.

One unexpected outcome of Thomas Melton's faithful obedience to God's calling was a family legacy of preaching the gospel. One of his sons, Marvin "Bus" Melton, founded a church and began a radio program focused on prayer. One of Thomas's grandsons became a traveling evangelist like his grandfather—only without a horse.

A century later, Thomas's legacy of evangelism continues with his great-granddaughter Joy Trachsel. She not only shares the gospel through books and blogs, she also tells others about Jesus through her ongoing podcast. The modes of delivery may be different today, but Jesus' life-saving message has not changed since Thomas first straddled a horse.

READ ROMANS 10:9-15 AND REFLECT: What are the consequences if we fail to tell others about Jesus' saving grace? Do you know someone who needs to hear about Jesus today?

Father, I am thankful to be one of your children, and I want to be a diligent witness for you. Make me and my family aware of opportunities to share Jesus with those who don't know him. Help us to show your love in word and deed. In Jesus' name, amen.

Legacy Tip

Foster in your children a burden for the spiritually lost. Help them understand the eternal consequences for people who don't know Jesus as their Savior. Pray regularly as a family for those you know who need salvation. Encourage your children to tell friends and family about their relationship with Jesus.

Genealogy Tip

WHEN YOU HIT A DEAD END

It happens to every researcher. You were researching one particular ances-tor's direct line and you hit a dead end. In that case, triangulation could help. Triangulation is a research strategy that uses multiple sources of data.[32] Before heading off in this new direction, first make sure you've exhausted every possibility. If you believe you have, then collect details from that ancestor's relatives who are matched to you on genealogical sites such as Ancestry, 23andMe, Family Tree, or My Heritage, among others. You can compare their family tree in order to draw conclusions about your ancestor's life events. Take a closer look at your ancestor's sib-lings, spouse, and children. Note dates, relationships, and significant life events to uncover additional clues to push forward on the study of your original ancestor.

37 | One Mother's Sacrifice

> *God said, "I will be with you. And this will be the sign to you that it is I who have sent you: When you have brought the people out of Egypt, you will worship God on this mountain."*
>
> EXODUS 3:12

Hudson Taylor was seventeen years old when he felt called to the mission field in China. But it wasn't surprising to his mother, Amelia. God had placed the desire on her heart years earlier. When Hudson was just a newborn, Amelia Taylor began praying that God would send her son to China as a missionary.[33] Amelia saw a great spiritual need in that vast and far-off country, and she longed for God to use her son to meet it, even though it would mean separation from him.

When Hudson left England in 1853 at the age of twenty-one, only a few dozen missionaries were in China. The country was virtually untouched by the gospel, a nation of souls held captive by sin. Burdened by their need, Hudson devoted his life to taking the gospel of Christ to that country.

Hudson served God there for more than fifty years, from 1853 until his death in 1905. Through the mission organization he founded, China Inland Mission, he established twenty mission stations, brought almost a thousand missionaries to China's interior, and trained seven hundred native workers. His efforts reaped an abundant spiritual harvest, including a strong Chinese church of around 125,000 believers.[34]

God used one mother's sacrifice to help save countless souls in China. In a similar way, God used another mother's sacrifice to free the people of Israel from slavery in Egypt. Jochebed (Exodus 6:20) carried out a strategic plan to save her son Moses from Pharaoh's cruel edict. She gave up her son to save his life and God's people. She trusted God with Moses' future, just as Amelia Taylor entrusted her son and his future to God.

The Lord chooses to work through people to carry out his redemptive purposes. In the lives of Hudson Taylor and Moses, God worked through a mother to prepare a deliverer. God still works this way today. Parents and grandparents can further God's purposes by encouraging their children to go wherever he calls.

READ EXODUS 1:22, 2:1-10, AND 3:12 AND REFLECT: What did Jochebed give up in order to save her son for God's purposes? In what ways do you see God's hand in this situation? According to Exodus 3:12, what was God's purpose for Moses?

> *Father, I want my family to seek your will in all things. Guide our conversations and give me the right words to encourage them to follow you no matter the cost. In Jesus' name, amen.*

Legacy Tip

Pray regularly with your children and ask God to give you wisdom regarding his will for them. Help your children recognize God's voice and discern his direction for their lives today and in the future. Encourage them to obey him, even if it means giving up financial success and comfort.

Genealogy Tip

MAKE THE MOST OF FAMILY REUNIONS

Do you tend to avoid family reunions? Make plans to attend the next one! These gatherings provide a wonderful opportunity to further your research. If a reunion is coming up, organize a genealogy presentation to celebrate your ancestors. Ask members of each family line to bring their ancestral photos, old letters, family Bibles, and other relevant items. Display these items with an enlarged multigenerational genealogy chart. Take photos of interesting items to aid in your own research. And spend time chatting with the oldest family members present. Pick their brains for any information or stories about your ancestors.

38 Power of the Pen

I will make every effort to see that after my departure you will always be able to remember these things.

2 PETER 1:15

He wrote countless books and curricula, all with the same goal: to make the Bible and Bible study accessible to everyone.

Jesse Lyman Hurlbut was born in New York City in 1843. After graduating from Wesleyan University in 1864, he became a pastor in the American Methodist Episcopal Church. Jesse served in several churches throughout New Jersey over the next two decades.[35] At that point he left the pastorate to take a position with his denomination's Sunday school organization. Jesse quickly became a prominent leader in the Sunday school movement of the late nineteenth and early twentieth centuries.

Whatever his title or role, Jesse devoted his life to teaching God's Word and ensuring the availability of a biblical education for young and old alike. He wrote material that instructed youth and equipped teachers on subjects such as church history, the life of Jesus, and the geography of the Holy Land. He did a series of Bible lessons for children and a bedtime Bible storybook. One of his most popular books is *Hurlbut's Story of the Bible for Young and Old*. This much-loved classic tells the complete chronological story of the Bible in 168 stand-alone stories. Jesse's work clearly, simply, and accurately presents solid biblical truth, and many of his writings and books are still available today.[36]

Jesse and his wife, Mary, had seven children, four of whom survived to adulthood. The youngest, Bertha Grace Hurlbut Dougherty, became a prominent artist and was the great-grandmother of Joanne Hagemeyer. Joanne, inspired by her ancestor Jesse Hurlbut's life work, uses her pen and her tongue to teach, mentor, and train others in God's Word. She writes Bible studies and teaches God's Word at women's retreats and events. Joanne often reflects on Jesse's legacy and prays that God will also use her to influence a new generation of people who love Scripture.

READ 2 PETER 1:12-15 AND REFLECT: What were Peter's priorities for the believers as he neared the end of his life? In what ways did he share God's truth with them? What do you want to leave behind as a legacy for your family? Are you living in such a way that you can do that?

Jesus, thank you for all the resources available today that make the Bible come alive for me and my family. Help us to have good conversations about how we are applying your truths in our lives. In Jesus' name, amen.

Legacy Tip

Determine what legacy you want to leave your family and develop a purposeful plan to make it happen. For instance, if you want your children to fall in love with God's Word, share Scripture with them in an appealing way. One potential strategy is to find a solid, engaging Bible storybook to read during nightly bedtime routines.

Genealogy Tip

DIRECT EVIDENCE IS ALWAYS BEST

Want to establish facts about an ancestor? Look for direct evidence. Vital records such as birth certificates, marriage licenses or certificates, and death certificates are examples of direct evidence. Indirect evidence would be hints you might find in documents uncovered in genealogical searches. For example, suppose you find the same surname as your ancestor on a land record for an adjoining property. While these two people with the same last name are likely related, a land record does not prove these relationships. Direct evidence is always better than indirect evidence.

God's greatness

PSALMS 96-99.

shew forth his salvation from day to day.
3 Declare his glory among the heathen, his wonders among all people.
4 For the LORD is great, and greatly to be praised: he is to be feared above all gods.
5 For all the gods of the nations are idols: but the LORD made the heavens.
6 Honour and majesty

11 Light is sown for the rig gladness for the upright in h
12 Rejoice in the LORD, ye and give thanks at the rem his holiness.

PSALM 9

A Psalm.

SING

Exhortation to

PSALM

PSALM 100.

A Psalm of praise.

MAKE a joyful noise unto the LORD, all ye lands.
2 Serve the LORD with gladness: come before his presence with

39 Through the Worst of Times

My brothers and sisters, you whom I love and long for, my joy and crown, stand firm in the Lord in this way, dear friends!

PHILIPPIANS 4:1

War shakes a man's faith. Without a solid foundation and encouragement to stand firm, it can even shatter it completely. Jean Grace Elliot never went to a war zone, but she served in the trenches alongside the young men she'd taught in Sunday school.

Jean loved helping others learn, first as a schoolteacher, then as a principal. But Jean's lifelong passion was teaching the Bible. Each week in Sunday school, Jean taught a group of boys—including her own three sons—how to love and follow Jesus Christ. As the years went by, the lads she discipled grew into teenagers, then young men.

When World War II broke out, her sons and several of her "boys" enlisted in the armed forces. These young men may have left Toronto to serve their country, but Jean did not leave them. She faithfully wrote letters to each of them. She even corresponded with one soldier while he was imprisoned in a German concentration camp. Jean filled her letters with Scripture to bolster their faith and encouraged them to stand firm in Christ. She prayed that their commitment to God would not simply survive in those desperate times, but that it would thrive.

Jean's efforts bore fruit. Later in life, she received many written expressions of gratitude from her "boys" for being a devoted teacher and encourager. Although Jean passed away in 1963 at the age of seventy-seven, her legacy of unshakable faith lives on in her students, her own children, and their children.

Jean followed the example of the apostle Paul. In his letter to the persecuted believers in Philippi, Paul encouraged them to cling to Christ no matter what circumstances they were enduring. Paul knew suffering, but he also knew that the strength and comfort of Christ was more than sufficient. No matter the struggle, no matter the outcome on this earth, believers can experience rock-solid faith, even through the worst of times.

READ PHILIPPIANS 1:27-30 AND REFLECT: According to Paul, what does it look like to live a life "worthy of the gospel of Christ" (verse 27)? How can you model this kind of unshakable faith in the midst of difficult circumstances? What are some tangible ways you and your family can stand firm in struggles?

Father, when my family and I encounter trials, remind us of your truth. You see us, you care for us, and you never stop working on our behalf, even when we can't readily see the evidence. Thank you for your presence to sustain us in hard times. In Jesus' name, amen.

Legacy Tip

When we experience tough times, our emotions can overshadow God's truth. Make a list of biblical truths to keep on hand for the difficult days when you and your family will need them. Include Scriptures about God's power, sovereignty, love, and concern for all your needs. Also add passages about how God uses trials to grow a believer's faith.

Genealogy Tip

WHEN TO HIRE A PROFESSIONAL GENEALOGIST

Is it time for professional help? If you've hit a wall in your research or are encountering challenges in interpreting your documentation, consider contacting a professional genealogist. But before you do, check their qualifications. A weekend genealogist who traces their roots on ancestry websites may not be equipped to tackle your specific case. Before you hire anyone, ask to see his or her credentials and fee schedule. Review samples of their past projects to make sure the quality of their work meets your expectations. Discuss with them the goals you have for the research and what sort of information you hope to gain from the final results.

That Will Leave a Mark

When your children ask their fathers in times to come, "What do these stones mean?" then you shall let your children know, "Israel passed over this Jordan on dry ground." For the LORD your God dried up the waters of the Jordan for you until you passed over.

JOSHUA 4:21-23, ESV

Every family has stories that begin with "Remember when . . ." In Mary's family, some favorite stories begin like this: "Remember when Sarah got stuck in a turnstile?" "Remember when we lost Sarah at Disney World?" Yes, several of Mary's memorable family events feature Sarah in a tight spot.

But Mary also has many family stories that feature God's activity in their lives. Her favorite is when God began bringing adults to their church, people who had never attended a church service before and knew nothing about the Bible. With God's leading, Mary and her husband started a Bible study for spiritual seekers, and God used that group to bring dozens of adults to faith in Christ.

As a permanent reminder of God's work, they bought a print depicting Jesus as the Good Shepherd who seeks and finds the one lost sheep. Their children know this story well, and every time someone else asks about the picture, they happily tell it again.

Mary's picture of Jesus is an example of a spiritual marker that commemorates a great activity of God. Not only does a special item help those who experienced God's intervention to personally remember it, the tangible memento also gives descendants a way to participate in these mighty works of God through hearing the story.

God established this principle of spiritual markers. When his people crossed the Jordan River on dry ground at flood stage, he directed them to set up memorial stones to preserve and pass down this story of his glorious intervention. The solid, physical reminders prompted questions from future generations who did not witness the miracle.

Sadly, memories can be short, and significant moments are often forgotten. Spiritual markers not only strengthen memory, they provide a great opportunity to pass down God stories to the next generation. If you don't tell your children what God has done in your life, who will?

READ JOSHUA 4:1-10 AND REFLECT: Why did God direct Joshua to set up memorial stones? How would the memorial impact future generations? Why is it important for your family to know and keep telling your God stories?

Father, I am amazed and humbled at how you work in my life and in the lives of my family. Help us not forget the miracles you've performed— big and small. May we never tire of telling the stories of your power and love. In Jesus' name, amen.

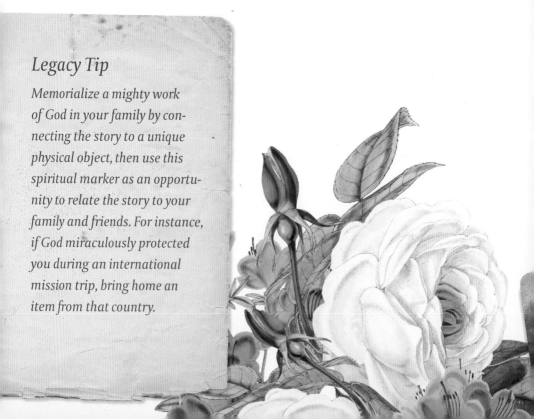

Legacy Tip

Memorialize a mighty work of God in your family by connecting the story to a unique physical object, then use this spiritual marker as an opportunity to relate the story to your family and friends. For instance, if God miraculously protected you during an international mission trip, bring home an item from that country.

Genealogy Tip

CONFLICTING INFORMATION

Are you frustrated because you're finding inconsistent details for the same ancestor? Unfortunately, conflicting information is common, particularly regarding birth dates. Prior to the twentieth century, widespread illiteracy left many with only a vague idea of when they were born. Therefore, they might note different dates on various forms. They could shift their birth date a bit if it benefited them. For instance, a woman who wanted to appear younger might record an earlier birth year on a marriage certificate. And a young man anxious to "escape the farm" by enlisting in the armed services might make himself appear older by writing down an earlier birth date on a military form. Keeping careful records and questioning all sources of information will help you sort out conflicting data as you research your family history.

41 They Took It to the Mountains

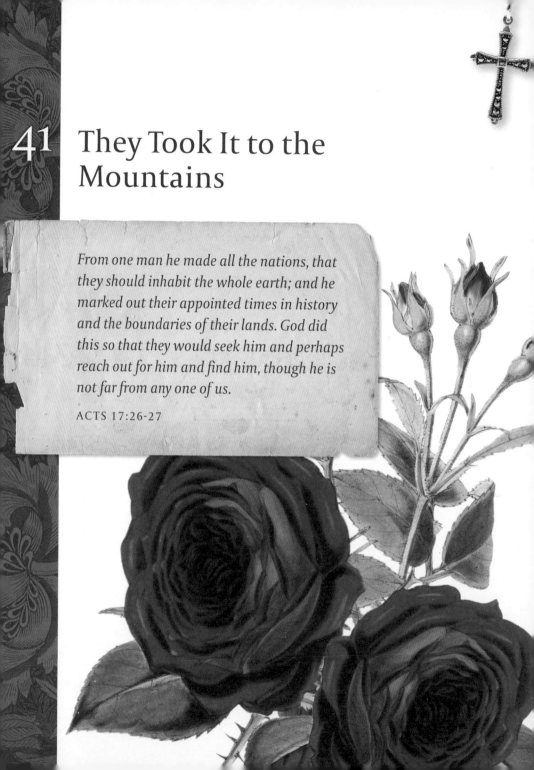

From one man he made all the nations, that they should inhabit the whole earth; and he marked out their appointed times in history and the boundaries of their lands. God did this so that they would seek him and perhaps reach out for him and find him, though he is not far from any one of us.

ACTS 17:26-27

Julie's family roots run deep through the Appalachian Mountains. Her mountain story begins with John Lilly, who sailed from England and arrived in the American colonies in 1633. He settled in Virginia and became a gentleman viewer of tobacco, an official who assessed the quality of the product before export.[37] Over the next century, John's descendants trickled into West Virginia and Kentucky, many moving deeper into areas secluded from the more civilized colonies.

In 1798, Thomas Lilly and his new wife, Rosana, settled on Bear Wallow Ridge along the Bluestone River in what is now West Virginia. Far up in the mountains, the couple raised eleven children. In such an isolated area separated from outsiders, many might assume even the gospel couldn't penetrate. But this family's story shows how God's plan for humankind knows no barriers.

Thomas and Rosana's son Robert became an itinerant preacher who took the gospel to other unreached settlers in the mountains. Everyone knew him as "Bear Wallow Bob." Bob's sister Juda married a godly man named Josiah, who also became a minister. In addition to raising twelve children, they also birthed the Bluestone Baptist Church. The church building may have been a log cabin with a dirt floor, but the salvation message was the same Good News heard in the grandest cathedrals of Europe.

Julie's Appalachian ancestors experienced the truth that Paul shared with ancient Greek philosophers in Athens: God is sovereign over all history, nations, and places. He works through every circumstance to make himself known. No place or people group is beyond the reach of his grace.

READ ACTS 17:24-28 AND REFLECT: In what ways does God work through human history to bring people to himself? How has he worked to draw you closer to himself? Based on this passage, what is God's ultimate desire for your children?

Father, I am thankful that my family members are expressing an interest in you. Open their eyes to help them see how much you are involved in and around their lives. Bring each of them to saving faith in Christ. In his name, amen.

Legacy Tip

Don't keep your "God story" to yourself. Let your family know how God first became real to you, how you found saving faith in Christ, and how he directs you today. Then ask them how God is working in their lives.

Genealogy Tip

DNA TESTING

Your ancestors left their mark on you. DNA testing, which analyzes a person's genetic makeup, can reveal close family relationships. Genealogists use three primary types of DNA tests to prove these connections, each one examining a different part of the human genome. Mitochondrial DNA traces the DNA passed from a mother to her children. Autosomal tests confirm relationships and ethnicity in both males and females. And the Y-DNA test focuses on the Y-chromosomes passed from father to son, which do not change over time. With the Y-DNA test, a male individual can trace his male ancestry up through many generations. Since females don't have Y chromosomes, this test can only gather information on direct paternal lines.

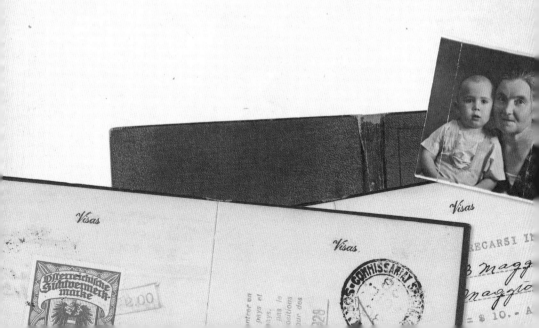

42 Model Student

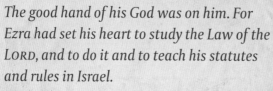

The good hand of his God was on him. For Ezra had set his heart to study the Law of the LORD, and to do it and to teach his statutes and rules in Israel.

EZRA 7:9-10, ESV

Don't talk with your mouth full. Obey the speed limit. Make your bed.

What do these statements have in common? They're all things parents teach their children to do but don't necessarily do themselves. At least not all the time.

To some degree or another, most parents have fallen into the trap of "Do as I say, not as I do." Although we think certain behaviors are good for our children, we may not value them enough to actually practice them. Unfortunately, this parenting method falls short. The living example will always be a louder teacher than words. Our actions reveal what we value most.

Telling children to base their lives on God's Word is far easier than putting it into practice for them every day. But if we long for our families to experience the joy and blessing of living a life that pleases God, they need a real-life model. They need someone to show them how it's done.

Ezra, a Jewish priest and scribe, taught God's Word to God's people. But before he taught God's law, he firmly resolved to learn it and apply it to his own life. He lived what he taught, showing his students how much he valued what God said. Ezra was a living, breathing object lesson.

Before you can effectively teach God's Word to your children, you have to live it. And before you can live it, you have to know it. When parents make reading and studying God's Word a priority, their children notice. When they see you open your Bible, when they watch you obediently follow God, they'll know you aren't all talk. Your genuine love for him will make a lasting impression.

READ EZRA 7:1-10 AND REFLECT: According to verse 9, what was one incredible result of Ezra's devotion to God's Word? If you commit to studying and obeying God's Word, what results might take place in your family?

> *Father, I commit myself to being in the Bible regularly. As I read and study, give me a deep love for Scripture that flows naturally into my daily life. May my commitment spark a flame of desire for you and your Word. In Jesus' name, amen.*

Legacy Tip

The way you live speaks more loudly than your words. Strive to read and study God's Word daily. Your passion will be contagious.

Genealogy Tip

LETTERS THAT CONTAIN QUESTIONABLE INFORMATION

Everybody has a few black sheep in their family tree. But few want others to know the details. Before sharing digitized letters or postcards online, review the content carefully for any sensitive information. Letters that contain gossip, offensive language, accounts of illicit behavior, or information that the original letter-writer may have considered confidential could cause embarrassment to the living descendants. Pause before you share documents that describe activities like drunkenness, extramarital affairs, unlawfulness, and similar kinds of behavior. A good guideline would be not to share anything you wouldn't want your descendants to know about you. Historical distance doesn't always remove the stigma of bad behavior.

God's greatness

PSALMS 96-99.

shew forth his salvation from day to day.

3 Declare his glory among the heathen, his wonders among all people.

4 For the LORD is great, and greatly to be praised: he is to be feared above all gods.

5 For all the gods of the nations are idols: but the LORD made the heavens.

6 Honour and

11 Light is sown for the rig gladness for the upright in h

12 Rejoice in the LORD, ye and give thanks at the rem his holiness.

PSALM 9
A Psalm.

O SING

Exhortation to

PSALM

PSALM 100.
A Psalm of praise.

MAKE a joyful noise unto the LORD all ye lands.

2 Serve the LORD with gladness: com before his presence with

She Trusted God

Blessed is the one who trusts in the LORD,
whose confidence is in him.

JEREMIAH 17:7

God powerfully used American evangelist D. L. Moody. Over his lifetime, it is estimated D. L. traveled more than a million miles, preaching to more than 100 million people.[38] But it was his mother who first taught him to trust in God.

Dwight Lyman Moody was born in Northfield, Massachusetts, in 1837 to Edwin and Betsey Moody. He was the sixth of nine children. Edwin, a bricklayer, died suddenly when D. L. was just four, leaving the family in deep debt. The creditors wasted no time in taking everything the law allowed, including the woodpile.

When friends encouraged Betsey to send some of the children to relatives, she refused. Determined to keep her family together, Betsey plowed the ground, planted crops, and sought work from neighbors to meet their needs.[39] Through many desperate times, God always miraculously provided. And Betsey learned he was trustworthy.

At age seventeen, D. L. left home to work in his uncle's Boston shoe store. There he attended Sunday school, where he learned more about God's love for him. With his Sunday school teacher's encouragement, he joyfully gave his life to Jesus. At nineteen, Moody moved to Chicago to pursue business endeavors.[40] But God had other plans for him.

Over the next several years, D. L.'s faith and evangelistic fervor grew. In 1858, he established a mission church in a Chicago slum, and by 1861, he entered full-time ministry.[41] God was building on the foundation of faith his mother laid.

When Betsey died, D. L. spoke at her funeral. He reflected on her determination to keep their family intact and how she nurtured him and his siblings spiritually with devotions every morning and church every Sunday. He shared her simple but profound creed: "My trust is in God."

Betsey encountered severe difficulties in her life. Many times she didn't know what form the help would take, but she always knew who would send it.

READ JEREMIAH 17:5-8 AND REFLECT: Do you ever look to people or things to provide what you need in times of difficulty? The last time you encountered a trial, where did you go first for help? How can you build your trust in God alone?

Father, I long for my family to always go to you first when difficulty hits, to rely on your counsel and direction. Draw me closer to you so I can effectively lead the way for them. In Jesus' name, amen.

Legacy Tip

When your family members encounter a difficulty, take the opportunity to point them to God. As they walk through the trial, keep encouraging them to trust in him. Teach them that God is always trustworthy.

Genealogy Tip

THE IMPORTANCE OF USING CITATIONS

Check your sources and provide your sources for others to check. When you come across information shared online by another researcher, look for citations—that's the best way to check the authenticity of information. If a document doesn't link to a citation, its validity may be in question. Likewise, if you plan to share genealogical information online with other researchers, include your sources in a footnote. It's good practice to clearly indicate where you found your information, especially when you're posting it for others to see. Do your best to find and share reliable content.

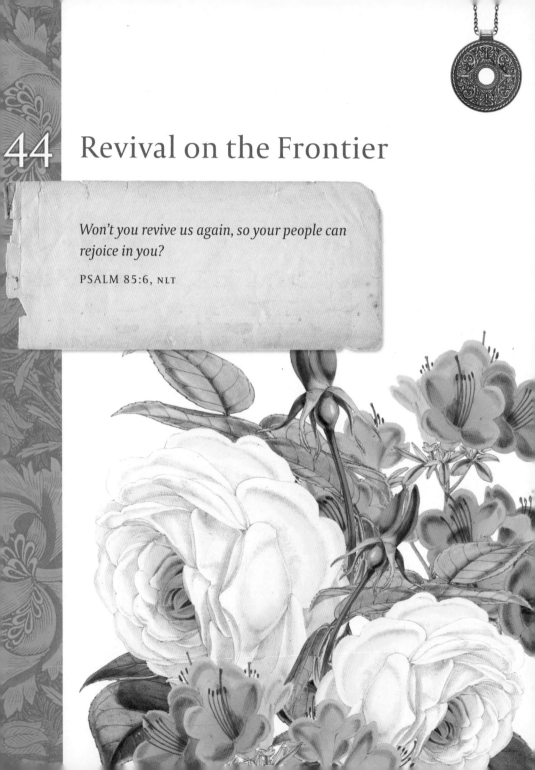

44 Revival on the Frontier

Won't you revive us again, so your people can rejoice in you?

PSALM 85:6, NLT

America's victory over the British in the Revolutionary War birthed a new nation. Yet it wasn't long before colonists and settlers on the American frontier experienced a period of significant moral depravity. With their livelihoods gone and their property ravaged from war, many people turned away from God and embraced false ideas about his character and nature. Large groups of people migrated to places like the wilds of western Kentucky and Tennessee looking for farmland and a fresh start. Sadly, murder, gambling, prostitution, and drunkenness were more prevalent than law and order. Something extraordinary needed to happen.to turn the country around.

Between 1795 and 1835, many communities held religious revivals. Evangelists including Presbyterian minister James McGready helped establish a camp known as the Red River Meeting House in Logan County, Kentucky (otherwise known as "Satan's Stronghold"). Frontier families traveled for miles to join the meetings, where they heard powerful preaching and engaged in fervent prayer. According to one witness, "Sinners [were] dropping down on every hand, shrieking, groaning, crying for mercy, convoluted. Professors [were] praying, agonizing, fainting, falling down in distress for sinners, or in raptures of joy." It was like the clouds opened and God's mercy flowed down on the people. The Second Great Awakening in America was underway.[42]

Becky's fourth great-grandfather, Reverend Francis Fielding Smith, who lived approximately twenty miles from the Red River Meeting House, was said to have preached at the camp. A tribute published in the Cumberland Presbyterian (April 8, 1835) after Reverend Smith's passing described his zeal for God as being so great he moved his wife and children to the encampment in order to support the worshiping assembly. The minister was concerned especially for his ten children, who were all "on the road to ruin." When the camp meetings were over, seven of them became professing members of the Cumberland Presbyterian Church. One of them eventually became a distinguished minister of the gospel. His determination to introduce his entire family to God's saving grace of salvation bore fruit.

When Becky learned about her great-grandfather's involvement in the Second Great Awakening, she visited the Red River Meeting House, where people still worship and pray. That trip renewed her passion for sharing the gospel message with family members. Like Francis Fielding Smith, she longs for the day when the whole family will be gathered for all of eternity with their heavenly Father.

READ PSALM 85:4-9 AND REFLECT: Are there any areas of sin or disobedience in your life creating a barrier between you and God? Confess them to him and ask him to revive and strengthen your relationship.

Father, you are merciful and forgiving. You long to restore those who wander from you. Show me every area of my life that displeases you. Revive my love and passion for you. In Jesus' name, amen.

Legacy Tip

The attitudes and behaviors accepted by culture are often opposed to what God wants for you and your family. Take every opportunity to show your children where the "normal" behavior of the world conflicts with God's standards. Also teach them about the need for repentance when they compromise with the world.

Genealogy Tip

PATRIOTIC AND LINEAL SOCIETIES

If you want to connect with others who share your passion for genealogy, consider joining a lineage society. There are hundreds of patriotic and lineal societies throughout the world, each one honoring an individual or a historical event. Membership requires documentation to prove the proper ancestral connection. Through these societies, members can converse with like-minded people and learn about "all things genealogy." The largest and most popular lineage societies in the United States are the Daughters of the American Revolution, Sons of the American Revolution, General Society of Mayflower Descendants, and the Order of the Crown of Charlemagne. Not only will membership enrich your genealogical interest, most of these societies have helpful records to aid in your research.

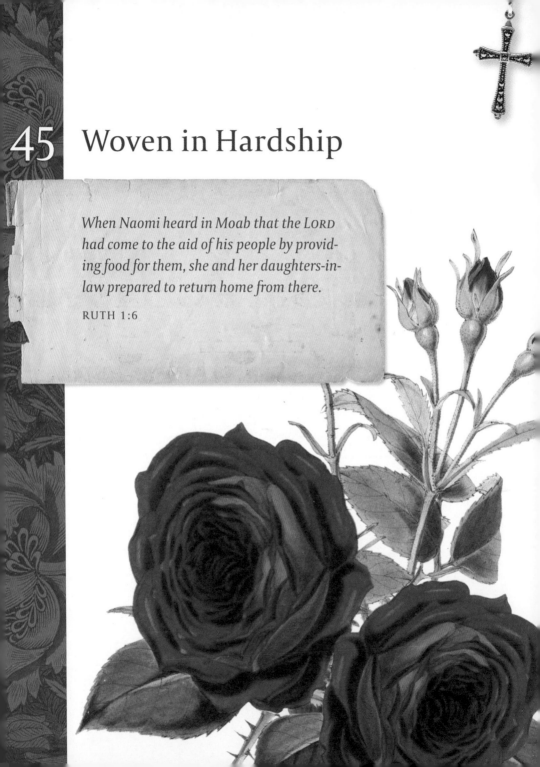

45 | Woven in Hardship

*When Naomi heard in Moab that the L*ORD *had come to the aid of his people by providing food for them, she and her daughters-in-law prepared to return home from there.*

RUTH 1:6

Naomi had lost everything. But in spite of her seemingly hopeless circumstances, she clung to her faith.

This Jewish wife and mother lived in Bethlehem during the time of the judges. When famine struck, the family moved to Moab. But trouble followed. First Naomi's husband, Elimelek, died. Then her two sons, Mahlon and Kilion, who had married Moabite women, also died. Naomi was a childless widow, which was a hopeless situation for a woman in the ancient world. Living in a foreign land with no one to depend on was a recipe for poverty and destitution.

Devastated, Naomi clung to her one remaining hope—God. When word reached Naomi that the Lord was providing food for his people in the land of Judah, she set out for home. Naomi purposefully moved closer to God when her circumstances were the gravest. She knew that he would give her strength. So she put herself in his hands, placing herself under his care and protection.

Naomi urged her daughters-in-law to stay in Moab, where they could remarry and start families. But Ruth refused to leave Naomi. She committed herself to Naomi and to Naomi's God (Ruth 1:16-18). Where did Ruth learn faith such as this? She saw it lived out in the life of her mother-in-law. Naomi demonstrated a faith worth having—relevant faith that gave her hope when her circumstances seemed hopeless. Ruth saw that and wanted it for herself.

In Ruth 4:13-17 we learn the rest of the story. Back in Bethlehem, God provided food and a home for Naomi and Ruth. He provided a husband for Ruth and a grandchild for Naomi. Naomi's unwavering trust in God wove a cord of faith that ran through Ruth. This faith cord joined with Boaz, then ran through their son to David and on to Jesus.

Let us choose faith like Naomi's. When trouble hits, may we trust in

God. Hardship strengthens and builds our faith as we receive God's love and reflect it to everyone around us. Our commitment to follow Jesus will be a cord of faith that runs through those who come after us.

READ RUTH 4:13-17 AND REFLECT: How do you respond when you encounter difficulties? What are some practical ways you can demonstrate unwavering faith to your loved ones? Reflect on how God has brought you through past trials and thank him for working in and through your life.

Father God, help me to trust in you when my circumstances seem hopeless. May my commitment to follow you amid my struggles be an unwavering testimony to those watching my life. In Jesus' name, amen.

Legacy Tip

Your family will experience heartache in this life. Prepare them for future struggles by sharing your own stories about how God has walked with you through trials. When members of your family encounter difficulties, show them how to cling to God's promises of comfort, peace, and strength.

Genealogy Tip

ASIAN MIGRATION

Until 1965, United States immigration policy favored European immigrants. But that changed when President Lyndon B. Johnson signed the 1965 Immigration and Nationality Act. This new law, also known as the Hart-Celler Act, abolished the national origins quota system that had vastly limited immigrants from Asian and Arab countries. The Hart-Celler Act busted the stranglehold of the restrictive, race-based immigration policies of the past. This radical move, which reflected the civil-rights climate of the country, opened the door for a major influx of emigrants from Asia. Before then, Asians accounted for about 5 percent of immigrants to the United States. Within a few short decades, Asians comprised about 25 percent of immigrants.[43]

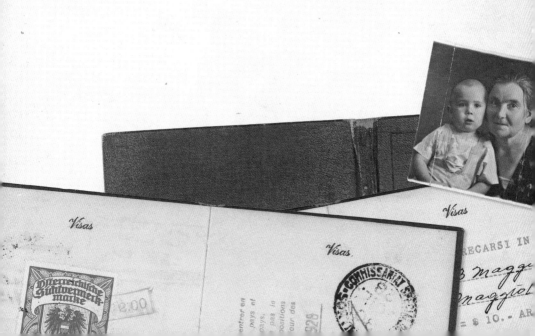

46 Farm Chores, Hymns, and Hiding God's Word

Let the words of my mouth and the meditation of my heart be acceptable in your sight, O LORD, my rock and my redeemer.

PSALM 19:14, ESV

Mary Hubbard grew up on a farm in Wisconsin, where the daily chores were far more than just staying on top of everything. Mary's mother, Amelia Dickau Hubbard, used them as opportunities for discipleship. While they worked together in the fields and milked the cows, Amelia taught Mary hymns. When they canned peaches and ironed clothes, Amelia recited Scripture and helped Mary memorize it.

Amelia, who had missed out on her own mother's discipleship, was committed to discipling her daughter. Although Amelia's mother taught her about God, Amelia was just ten when her mother passed away. God then used a godly Sunday school teacher to pick up where Amelia's mother had left off. The teacher helped foster her faith and encouraged Amelia to memorize God's Word.

In her later years, Amelia's church family called her "Mother Hubbard." It was a title of respect and fondness that they equated with her faithfulness to God. In addition to discipling her own daughter, Mother Hubbard also discipled countless other children through Sunday school classes. And Mother Hubbard always helped her students memorize a Bible verse each week. She firmly believed that memorizing Scripture was key to building and maintaining a strong faith. She taught her students and her daughter to hide God's Word in their hearts so that their words and thoughts would please God.

The Scriptures Mary learned as a child never left her. Even after her father's death, when she distanced herself from the Lord for a time, God's Word continued to minister to her heart, giving her strength and drawing her back. Looking back, Mary wishes she had discipled her own daughter more during that period away from God. Now, as Mary teaches and ministers to others, she always encourages them to memorize Scripture. And like Amelia, Mary helps her own daughter hide God's Word in her heart.

READ PSALM 19:7-14 AND REFLECT: What does this passage teach about the nature of God's Word? What impact does the Word have on a Christian's life? How would your children benefit from memorizing Scripture?

Lord God, your Word is sure, right, and true. Your Word imparts wisdom, joy, and insight. I want to hide your truths in my heart and always be ready to share them. Help me encourage my family to memorize Scripture too. In Jesus' name, amen.

Legacy Tip

Memorize Scripture as a family. Choose verses or passages based on your children's ages. Take advantage of daily moments to practice together, such as during car commutes. Keep track of everyone's progress with charts and stickers. Reward your children's success with something that motivates them.

Genealogy Tip

NAME CHANGES

Have you lost track of one particular ancestor? Look closely at his or her name. Is it possible it may have changed at some point? Tracing individuals or families who changed their names is a common occurrence in genealogical research. People who emigrated from other countries often changed their names after arriving in the United States. Many immigrants may simply have believed it would help them assimilate into their new culture. Others may have adopted an Americanized name to make it easier for others to pronounce. Often they believed the change would significantly increase their earning potential. When researching a surname, consider the original name that's behind the Americanized version, as well as its many spelling variations.

Unstoppable Joy

Rejoice inasmuch as you participate in the suffering of Christ, so that you may be overjoyed when his glory is revealed.

1 PETER 4:13

Peirina Giancarli possessed a deep and abiding joy in Christ despite her family's rejection and her husband's mistreatment. This exceptional joy—unstoppable even in the face of persecution—became a lasting heritage for those who came after her.

In 1923, Peirina and her infant daughter, Antonia, left their small village in the Sibillini Mountains of Italy and sailed to America. After entering the country through Ellis Island, they joined Peirina's husband, Francesco, in Chicago. He had sailed ahead of them to take a job at a commercial cement company owned by Peirina's brother. Times were hard in Italy, and jobs were scarce, but opportunity awaited them in America.

The family settled in Chicago, close to extended family, and soon the couple had two more daughters, Anna and Paula. They settled into their new home and made friends. One day a friend invited Peirina to a prayer meeting that changed the course of her life. For the first time, she heard about a personal, saving relationship with Jesus Christ. She received him with joy.

But Peirina's joy in Christ came at a great price. Francesco and her family didn't understand her choice and thought Peirina had lost her mind. Her extended family ostracized her. Francesco did everything he could to hinder his wife's new faith. He prohibited her from attending church and repeatedly burned her Bibles. But Peirina refused to reject Jesus. She locked herself in the bathroom to pray and stole away to the coal cellar to read and study her Bible. When possible, she attended church without Francesco's knowledge.

Francesco died at the age of fifty-four. After thirty-one years of marriage, Peirina was a widow. For the rest of her life she lived with Paula, Anna, and their respective families.

Throughout her years, Peirina clung to Christ. Despite her trials, God sustained her by his Spirit and blessed her with unstoppable joy. Peirina's remarkable faith left a lasting impression on her granddaughter, Anna's daughter Terri, who loved Nonna's daily time with God. Her prayers and her songs of worship were always fervent, always loud, and always in Italian. But Nonna's never-ending joy in Christ left the deepest mark on Terri. And every time she sees Nonna's Italian Bible sitting on the corner of her desk, Terri thanks God for her grandmother's legacy.

READ 1 PETER 4:12-16 AND REFLECT: According to Peter, what role does suffering have in a Christian's life? Why should persecution and trials be a reason for joy? In light of these truths, how should you respond to difficulty or persecution?

> *Father, give me courage when people shun or mock me for my beliefs. Refine and strengthen my faith when challenges come so I can be an example to my family. I am grateful that your Son died on the cross for me. That alone is a reason to be joyful. In his name, amen.*

Legacy Tip

Ask your family members to think of a time when they were ridiculed for their faith. Did they accept the criticism joyfully or angrily? Discuss the importance of responding with joy and thank God for his presence in the midst of difficult situations.

Genealogy Tip

THE PROPER WAY TO CLEAN A HEADSTONE

Headstones are a good source of key data on your ancestors. You'll want to protect that information for the generations to come. As tempting and noninvasive as it seems, do not make rubbings of the headstone. If you plan to clean or restore an ancestor's headstone, use a method that's safe for the marker. Pressure washers, wire or metal brushes, and harsh household cleaners will cause irreparable damage. According to preservation experts, many cleaners leave behind destructive salt deposits on the stone. Avoid cleaners that contain harsh chemicals like sodium sulfate, ammonium carbonate, sodium bicarbonate, sodium chloride, or sodium carbonate, which will corrode the stone and make your ancestor's marker unreadable. Instead, use a cleaner made especially for headstones and make sure you have access to plenty of water for rinsing.

48 Passing the Torch

My son Solomon, acknowledge the God of your father, and serve him with whole-hearted devotion and with a willing mind.... Consider now, for the LORD has chosen you to build a house as the sanctuary. Be strong and do the work.

1 CHRONICLES 28:9-10

It began in a tiny church in Saskatchewan, Canada. The church had dwindled to just ten souls when they called Henry Blackaby to be their pastor, and he left a large church in California to accept the call. Over the next twelve years, Henry and his family witnessed God do things that only God could do. The church grew into a vibrant, healthy congregation that planted thirty-eight mission churches and established a denominational seminary.[44]

Through this experience and his daily time with God in prayer and Bible study, Henry learned biblical truths that shaped his life and leadership. He later shared these spiritual principles in *Experiencing God: Knowing and Doing the Will of God*. Since its publication in 1990, the book has been translated into forty-five languages and sold more than seven million copies, impacting countless Christians for more than three decades.[45]

Today, all five of Henry and Marilyn Blackaby's children and many of their grandchildren serve in full-time ministry. Their eldest son, Richard Blackaby, is president of Blackaby Ministries International, which responds to the many ministry opportunities God has provided through the message of *Experiencing God*.[46] This family legacy began when one ordinary man made a commitment to know God and to do his will.

Another example of passing the torch of faith is found in 1 Chronicles. David, the shepherd boy who became king of Israel, is described as a man after God's own heart. He was not perfect, but he sought God and desired to follow his leading. And he longed for his son Solomon, the heir to the throne, to do the same. Near the end of his life, David challenged Solomon to embrace his spiritual heritage and serve God with his whole heart. That's a legacy worth passing down.

READ 1 CHRONICLES 28:1-10 AND REFLECT: In what ways would Solomon continue what his father began? What spiritual responsibility did David entrust to Solomon? What warning did David give his son? How can you intentionally and verbally encourage your children to live for God?

Father, I long for my children to walk closely with you. Help me to compose a spiritual challenge that will motivate them to always follow you. In Jesus' name, amen.

Legacy Tip

Craft a spiritual challenge for your children and grandchildren. Use the next gathering or holiday to share it with your family. Create a visual record of this commitment to serve as a constant and lasting reminder. Print it, frame it, and hang it where everyone can see it.

Genealogy Tip

KEEP ENHANCING YOUR EDUCATION

Do you want to learn more about genealogical research? Endless opportunities exist to educate yourself. Check public and university libraries, historical societies, and genealogical societies to find out what genealogical education they provide. Many offer free or low-cost seminars, presentations, and workshops on various historical topics. Libraries often have entire genealogy resource sections that are accessible to the public. In addition, many have volunteer genealogists on staff to provide guidance and suggestions for your research. Contact your local library for information about their genealogy program, as well as any available seminars or workshops.

Patriot of Faith

> *By faith the prostitute Rahab, because she welcomed the spies, was not killed with those who were disobedient.*
>
> HEBREWS 11:31

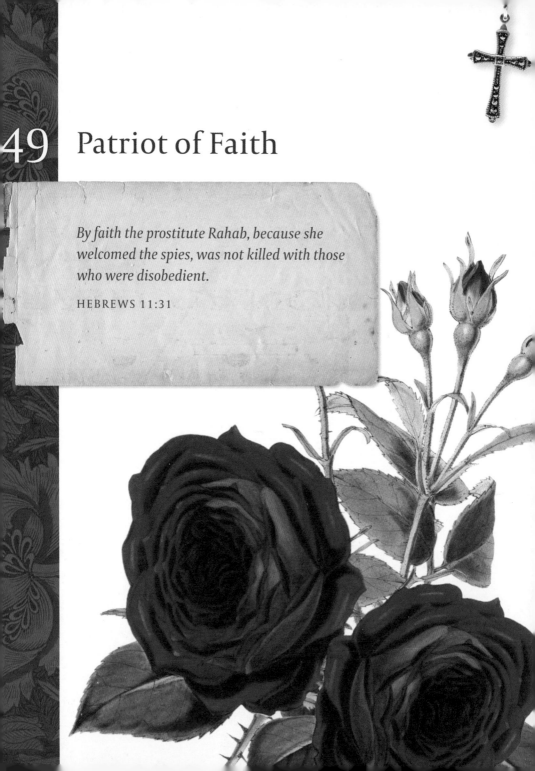

When Mary first embarked on the personal journey of ancestry research, she longed to learn when her ancestors first came to America. But the trails she found only led her deeper and deeper into her family's history in America. Then she discovered some unexpected—but not unwelcome—leaves on her family tree. One of Mary's ancestors fought in the Revolutionary War. She is descended from a patriot!

Mary's sixth great-grandfather Robert C. Chandler was born in New Kent County, Virginia, in 1729. During America's war for independence, Robert served as a private in the Virginia troops. Even though he wasn't leading soldiers into battle, Mary's ancestor helped win freedom for his country and the generations to follow.

The genealogy of Jesus also includes a few unexpected ancestors and at least one patriot of faith. Rahab (Matthew 1:5) was a Gentile pagan and prostitute living in the ancient city of Jericho when Israel's leader, Joshua, sent spies to scout out the city for invasion. The two Hebrew spies found lodging and refuge in Rahab's home in the city wall. But the king was searching for these men, and Rahab faced a life-altering decision—hide and protect the Hebrews or turn them over to the authorities.

Rahab—and everyone else in Jericho—had heard of the mighty miracles the Hebrews' God had performed. They feared his power. But only Rahab put her faith in him. When she chose to align herself with the Hebrew God and his people, she gave up her home, her community, and everything she knew. But her hard choice saved her life and the lives of her family.[47]

This courageous choice also charted a new course for Rahab and her descendants. It began a lineage of faith that flowed through her descendant Boaz (the husband of Ruth) to Jesse the father of David, and on through the generations to Joseph (the husband of Mary, the mother of Jesus). When Rahab cast her lot with the God of the Hebrews, her choice rippled through the centuries, impacting future generations all the way to Jesus, the Savior who won our eternal freedom.

READ JOSHUA 6:22-25 AND REFLECT: What was the result of Rahab's courageous choice for herself and her family? What hard choice can you make today that has the potential to positively impact the faith of your family tomorrow?

> *Father, sometimes it's hard to choose you and your purposes over the easier, more "acceptable" way. Give me strength and boldness to follow your path even when it's difficult. In Jesus' name, amen.*

Legacy Tip

If you have older children, talk with them about any important decision you must make that will affect the whole family, such as a move to another city. You can take the opportunity to show them how you seek and follow God's guidance. Follow up later and discuss the results of that hard but courageous choice.

Genealogy Tip

KISSING COUSINS

Are you concerned about finding cousins among the marital relationships on your family tree? There's no reason to worry. Through the nineteenth century, marriage between first cousins was legal and even common in both the United States and the United Kingdom. Since many communities were isolated, suitable marriage partners were limited. Also, marriage to a cousin did not carry the same stigma it does today. These matches were not only acceptable—they could even be beneficial. These unions helped keep wealth and property within the family.

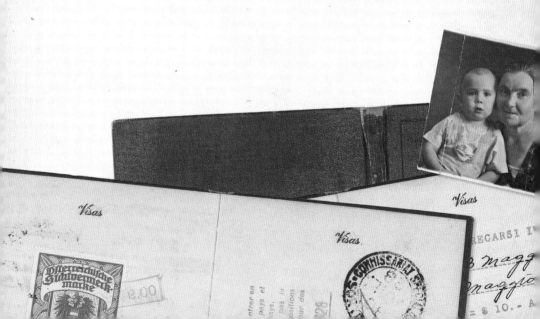

50 Grandkid Camp

I press on toward the goal to win the prize for which God has called me heavenward in Christ Jesus.

PHILIPPIANS 3:14

Yes, it's hard work. Yes, it's exhausting. Yes, it takes planning. But the fun and the results far exceed the effort.

Nancie and Bill have been hosting a two-day camp for their grandchildren for seventeen years. A total of fourteen children have participated. The couple's goals for Grandkid Camp include making memories, having fun, deepening family relationships, and helping their grandchildren grow in faith.

These fun grandparents build each year's camp around a theme. They've used exciting motifs such as *Star Wars*, the Olympics, and the Oregon Trail. The theme is the launchpad for food, games, crafts, and even Scripture memorization. For example, the verse they helped their grandkids memorize during the Olympics-themed camp was, "Do you not know that in a race all the runners run, but only one gets the prize? Run in such a way as to get the prize" (1 Corinthians 9:24).

Learning Scripture is always a key element of Grandkid Camp, because Nancie and Bill know its great spiritual value. Early in their marriage, when serving as youth pastors, they made this discipline a priority with the young people. Once the teens planted God's Word in their hearts, it stayed with them for a lifetime. Nancie and Bill want their grandchildren to experience that as well.

The effort required to make Grandkid Camp happen is definitely paying off. In addition to having an enjoyable time and memorizing verses, Nancie and Bill's grandkids are committing their lives to Jesus and growing spiritually. Two summers ago, during a family vacation at the lake, five of their grandsons professed their personal statements of faith and asked their grandparents to baptize them.

Nancie and Bill devote time, energy, creativity, and prayer to building a legacy of faith. Grandkid Camp is both the hardest and most rewarding

thing they've ever done, but their investment is reaping eternal results in their grandchildren.

READ PHILIPPIANS 3:7-14 AND REFLECT: What place did Jesus have in Paul's life? Can you honestly say that compared to your desire for Jesus, everything else is "worthless"? Is pursuing a close walk with Christ a priority in your life? What do you need to let go of in order to decisively pursue God's purpose for you?

Lord, give me the creativity and energy I need to make an eternal investment in the youngest members of my family. Help me "press on" and direct my kids or grandkids toward Jesus. In Jesus' name, amen.

Legacy Tip

Plan a weekend camp or day camp around a creative theme for your children or grandchildren. Make it fun, and include spiritual elements like Bible stories, prayer, and Scripture memorization.

Genealogy Tip

NEWSPAPERS

Newspaper archives can yield a wealth of information about your ancestors. Newspapers.com is a great starting point. Obituaries often include birth and death dates, place of birth and death, occupation, residency, and names of family members. And don't forget the society pages; social events such as weddings, engagements, anniversaries, and family reunions can aid your research. If a newspaper wasn't published in the location you're researching, try libraries in the closest large town or adjoining county. Libraries may have either microfilm or digitized archives of newspapers that have ceased publication.

God's greatness
PSALMS 96-99.

shew forth his salvation from day to day.
3 Declare his glory among the heathen, his wonders among all people.
4 For the LORD is great, and greatly to be praised: he is to be feared above all gods.
5 For all the gods of the nations are idols: but the LORD made the heavens.
6 Honour and

11 Light is sown for the rig
gladness for the upright in h
12 Rejoice in the LORD, ye
and give thanks at the rem
his holiness.

PSALM 9
A Psalm.

Exhortation to

PSALM

PSALM 100.
A Psalm of praise.

MAKE a joyful noise unto the LORD
all ye lands.
2 Serve the LORD with gladness:

51 Like Father, Like Daughters

On the next day we departed and came to Caesarea, and we entered the house of Philip the evangelist, who was one of the seven, and stayed with him. He had four unmarried daughters, who prophesied.

ACTS 21:8-9, ESV

Steve Irwin spent his life helping crocodiles. He and his family lived at the Australia Zoo, an expansion of the reptile park his parents had founded. Steve first learned about handling crocodiles from his father. Years later, a wildlife documentary introduced Steve to the world, and his expertise and natural charm made viewers want more. The result was *The Crocodile Hunter*, a wildly popular television series.

Steve's passion for wildlife conservation evolved into the "family business," which included his wife, Terri, daughter, Bindi, and even his young son, Robert. Before Robert was born, Bindi was her dad's constant companion, endearing her to fans. Sadly, in 2006, Steve was tragically killed by a stingray's barb to the chest. Today the Irwin family works tirelessly at keeping his legacy going, helping the animals he loved. Their television show, *Crikey! It's the Irwins*, continues to document their story while paying tribute to Steve.

Passion is contagious. When parents include their children in their service to God, the children often "catch" the same fervor, the same sense of purpose. Philip the evangelist and his daughters illustrate this well.

Philip was one of the first seven deacons in the early church. When Christian persecution heated up in Jerusalem, Philip went to Samaria to share the Good News of salvation. Many people believed his message and gave their lives to Jesus. Philip proclaimed the truth—that all people are spiritually lost and in need of a Savior, and that Jesus Christ is the Savior we need.

Philip's unmarried daughters caught their father's passion. The Bible tells us that all four "prophesied." They shared their father's calling of proclaiming the gospel. These young women had grown up hearing their father preach boldly to anyone who would listen, and now they couldn't

remain silent. Like father, like daughters. Just imagine what their family's dinner conversation must have sounded like!

READ ACTS 8:4-8, 12 AND 21:8-9 AND REFLECT: What do you think your children or grandchildren would say is your passion? Would their answer include anything about your service to God? Are you living out God's calling on your life in a way they can see?

Father, give me clear direction regarding the ways I should be serving you. Give me a passion for those purposes, and show me how I can include my family. In Jesus' name, amen.

Legacy Tip

Think of some ways your children or grandchildren can participate in what you're doing to serve God, your church, and your community. Give them age-appropriate ways to help. Or sit down as a family and decide on a new area of service that you can do together.

Genealogy Tip

MILITARY RECORDS

Do you want to research an ancestor who served in the United States military? The National Archives holds the best records for federal-level military service in the National Personnel Records Center: military personnel records. Before you dive in, gather all the facts you already know to aid your research. Information such as which military branch your ancestor served in, his or her dates of service, and any specific conflicts he or she fought in will help you make the best use of the records. Was the individual an officer or enlisted person? And did your ancestor apply for or receive a pension for his or her military service? The answers to those questions are beneficial. Now you can move forward—armed with the facts!

52 Celebrate Jesus

The shepherds returned, glorifying and praising God for all the things that they had heard and seen, as it was told unto them.

LUKE 2:20, KJV

A few years ago, while I was speaking at a ladies' Christmas event, something unexpected happened. I had planned to read portions of the Christmas story from Matthew and Luke. But as I began to read from my open Bible, I discovered I did not need it. The words flowed from memory—KJV style.

Here's the truly amazing part: I've never purposely memorized those sections of Scripture. The passages were embedded in my heart simply because my father read them to our family every Christmas Eve as part of our family celebration. My dad desired to keep our hearts and minds on the real meaning of Christmas. He felt the same way about Easter, Thanksgiving, and every other holiday. While he enjoyed the cultural aspects of these celebrations, he always honored God first and encouraged his family to do the same.

As our own children grew, my husband and I carried on that legacy. When our kids were old enough to understand, I began baking a birthday cake for Jesus on Christmas Eve. We even had candles and sang "Happy Birthday." It was a simple but effective way to help our children remember why we celebrate Christmas.

Jesus is the reason for the celebrations that fill Scripture. On one level, the feasts in the Old Testament, such as Passover and the Feast of Weeks, celebrate God's physical provision and miraculous deliverance. But ultimately they all point to the coming Savior and his provision of eternal life. Jesus also established another celebration. Until he returns, believers regularly partake of the Lord's Supper to remember Jesus' death and celebrate his resurrection.

As our families enjoy holidays and other special events, let's intentionally point them to Jesus. Let's make him the center of our days and the center of our families. Whatever else we may celebrate, let's acknowledge Jesus first. He gives us the reason to celebrate. Jesus *is* every reason to celebrate.

READ LUKE 2:8-20 AND REFLECT: What reasons did the shepherds have to rejoice and celebrate Jesus' birth? What reasons do you have to glorify and praise God because of Jesus? How can you encourage others to celebrate Jesus like the shepherds did that first Christmas?

> *Lord Jesus, you give us reason to celebrate every day. Show me how to consistently urge my family to remember you when we gather to enjoy holidays and family events.*

Legacy Tip

As each holiday and family get-together approaches, begin by preparing your own heart to celebrate Jesus. Then find creative ways to direct your family's attention to Jesus and his provision. For Thanksgiving, choose psalms that express gratitude to God and have family members read them at the dinner table. For Christmas, you might make a birthday cake for Jesus and add "Happy Birthday" to your song list of traditional carols.

Genealogy Tip

FAMILY BIBLES

If you have an old family Bible, you hold a true heirloom. Carefully check its pages for facts about your family. People of yesteryear often recorded significant life events—such as births, deaths, and marriages—on the Bible's opening pages. Many Bibles also contain written records of family trees. Families treasured these Bibles and passed them down from one generation to the next. If you don't have your family's heirloom Bible, check with a few of your relatives. In recent years, family Bible records have also been digitized. A good place to start searching for family Bible records is the historical society or library in the county in which your ancestor resided.

Notes ❧

1. Laurie Goodstein, "Billy Graham, 99, Dies; Pastor Filled Stadiums and Counseled Presidents," obituary in the *New York Times*, February 21, 2018, https://www.nytimes.com/2018/02/21/obituaries/billy-graham-dead.html.

2. Aaron Earls, "Billy Graham's Life & Ministry by the Numbers," LifeWay: *Facts & Trends*, February 21, 2018, https://factsandtrends.net/2018/02/21/billy-grahams-life-ministry-by-the-numbers/.

3. "7 Life Lessons Billy Graham Learned from His Mother," Billy Graham Evangelistic Association, May 4, 2018, https://billygraham.org/story/7-life-lessons-billy-graham-learned-from-his-mother/.

4. "German Immigrants," Immigration to the United States, accessed by Keith J. Bell via familysearch.org, November 29, 2020, https://www.immigrationtounitedstates.org/519-german-immigrants.html.

5. See "Immigration to the United States, 1851–1900," Library of Congress, accessed November 29, 2020, https://www.loc.gov/classroom-materials/united-states-history-primary-source-timeline/rise-of-industrial-america-1876-1900/immigration-to-united-states-1851-1900/.

6. Hasia Diner, "Immigration and Migration," The Gilder Lehrman Institute of American History, ap.gilderlehrman.org/essays/immigration-and-migration?period=6.

7. "Johann Peter Kichline, 1722–1789," http://www.kichline.com/genealogy/kichpete.htm.

8. S. M. Parkhill, "Peter Kichline Influenced Easton History," *The Morning Call*, July 30, 1998, https://www.mcall.com/news/mc-xpm-1998-07-30-3214899-story.html.

9. Parkhill, "Peter Kichline Influenced Easton History."

10. "389 Years Ago in 1629 …" Jamestowne Society, November 5, 2018, http://www.jamestowne.org/blog/389-years-ago-in-1629.

11. Hudson Valley Network, Inc., "Freer-Low Family Association," Historic Huguenot Street, huguenotstreet.org/freer.

12. Freer Family Genealogy Research, "Huguenot Freers," https://home.cc.manitoba.ca/~sfreer/huguenot.html.

13. Angela Boswell. "Married Women's Property Rights and the Challenge to the Patriarchal Order: Colorado County, Texas," in *Negotiating Boundaries of Southern Womanhood: Dealing With the Powers That Be*, Janet L. Coryell et al, ed. (Columbia, MO: University of Missouri Press, 2000), 92.

14. Library of Congress, Research Guides, American Women: Resources from the Law Library, State Law Resources, Property Law: Married Women's Property Laws, https://guides.loc.gov/american-women-law/state-laws#s-lib-ctab-19233885-1.

15. See history.com, U.S. Immigration Timeline, 1880, https://www.history.com/topics/immigration/immigration-united-states-timeline.

16. D. N. Freedman, ed., *The Anchor Yale Bible Dictionary*, vol. 2 (New York: Doubleday), 930.

17. Richard J. Leyda, "Henrietta Cornelia Mears," Database: Christian Educators of the 20th Century, Talbot School of Theology/Biola University, accessed November 29, 2020, https://www.biola.edu/talbot/ce20/database/henrietta-cornelia-mears.

18. Diana Lynn Severance, *Feminine Threads: Women in the Tapestry of Christian History* (Ross-shire, Scotland: Christian Focus Publications, 2011), 304.

19. Matt Brown, "The Hundred Year Influence of Henrietta Mears," August 3, 2018, CBN News, https://www1.cbn.com/cbnnews/cwn/2018/august/the-hundred-year-influence-of-henrietta-mears.

20. Will Graham, "The Tree Stump Prayer: When Billy Graham Overcame Doubt," July 9, 2014, Billy Graham Evangelistic Association, https://billygraham.org/story/the-tree-stump-prayer-where-billy-graham-overcame-doubt/.

21. Daphne Gentry, in the *Dictionary of Virginia Biography*, "Walter Chiles (1609–after July 6, 1653)," Encyclopedia Virginia, accessed November 29, 2020, https://www.encyclopediavirginia.org/Chiles_Walter_1609-after_July_6_1653#start_entry.

22. Martha W. McCartney, Jamestown People to 1800: Landowners, Public Officials, Minorities, and Native Leaders (Baltimore, MD: Genealogical Publishing Company, 2012), 112.

23. See Library of Virginia, Research Notes Number 30, "Lost Records Localities: Counties and Cities with Missing Records," accessed November 29, 2020, https://www.lva.virginia.gov/public/guides/rn30_lost records.pdf.

24. "The Wordless Book—Discover Its Rich Heritage," Our History, Child Evangelism Fellowship, https:// www.cefonline.com/about/history/wordless-book-discover-rich-heritage/.

25. "Fanny J. Crosby (March 24, 1820–February 12, 1915)," The Paperless Hymnal, http://www.paperless hymnal.com/tph/stories/fannyjcrosby/index.htm.

26. "Fanny Crosby: America's Hymn Queen," Timeline on Christianity.com, https://www.christianity.com /church/church-history/timeline/1801-1900/fanny-crosby-americas-hymn-queen-11630385.html.

27. "U.S., War Bounty Land Warrants, 1789–1858," https://www.ancestry.com/search/collections/1165/.

28. Diana Lynn Severance, Feminine Threads, 212.

29. Anne Adams, "Susanna Wesley: Mother of Methodism," History's Women, https://www.historyswomen .com/womenoffaith/SusannahWesley.html.

30. Severance, Feminine Threads, 214.

31. Historian, United Stated Postal Service, "Postal Service Mission and 'Motto,'" October 1999, https:// about.usps.com/who-we-are/postal-history/mission-motto.pdf.

32. Diahan Southard, "Tips for Triangulating Your DNA Matches," Family Tree magazine, familytree magazine.com/dna/triple-play-dna-matches-triangulation.

33. Mark Galli, ed., "Hudson Taylor: Faith Missionary to China," Christian History, issue 52, 1996, https://www .christianitytoday.com/history/people/missionaries/hudson-taylor.html.

34. Ed Reese, "James Hudson Taylor," originally published in Christian Hall of Fame series booklet (July 13, 1999), archived at Wholesome Words, https://www.wholesomewords.org/missions/biotaylor2.html.

35. Details of Reverend Jesse Lyman Hurlbut found at https://www.geni.com/people/Reverend-Jesse -Hurlbut/6000000018605674334.

36. Jesse Lyman Hurlbut Collection (12 vols.) available at https://www.logos.com/product/25315/jesse -lyman-hurlbut-collection.

37. "Viewers of Tobacco Crop, 1639," The Virginia Magazine of History and Biography, vol. 5, no. 2 (October 1897), 119–23, JSTOR, https://www.jstor.org/stable/4242027?seq=1#metadata_info_tab_contents.

38. George Thomas Kurian, ed., Nelson's Dictionary of Christianity (Nashville: Thomas Nelson, 2005), 472. See also "Dwight L. Moody: Did You Know?" Christian History, issue 25, 1990, https://www.christianitytoday .com/history/issues/issue 25/dwight-l-moody-dod-you-know.html.

39. Tim Challies, "The Power of a Hard-Working Mother (Christian Men and Their Godly Moms)," @ Challies, June 17, 2017, https://www.challies.com/articles/the-power-of-a-hard-working-mother/.

40. Challies, "The Power of a Hard-Working Mother (Christian Men and Their Godly Moms)."

41. Mark Galli, ed., "Dwight L. Moody: Revivalist with a Common Touch," Christian History, issue 25, 1990, https://www.christianitytoday.com/history/people/evangelistsandapologists/dwight-l-moody.html.

42. Mark Galli, "Revival at Cane Ridge," Christian History, issue 45, 1995, https://www.christianitytoday.com /history/issues/issue-45/revival-at-cane-ridge.html.

43. Muzaffar Chishti, Faye Hipsman, and Isabel Ball, "Fifty Years On, the 1965 Immigration and Nationality Act Continues to Reshape the United States," Migration Policy Institute, October 15, 2015, https://www .migrationpolicy.org/article/fifty-years-1965-immigration-and-nationality-act-continues-reshape -united-states.

44. Lee Weeks, "Grateful Friends Mark Henry Blackaby's 80th," Baptist Press, April 21, 2015, http://www .bpnews.net/44596/grateful-friends-mark-henry-blackabys-80th.

45. Weeks, "Grateful Friends Mark Henry Blackaby's 80th."

46. "Our Story," Blackaby Ministries International, accessed November 29, 2020, https://blackaby.org /about-blackaby-ministries-international/our-story/.

47. You can read the beginning of Rahab's story in Joshua 2 and the end of the story in Joshua 6:15-25.

My Legacy Story ❧